art / shop / eat
BERLIN

Simon Garnett

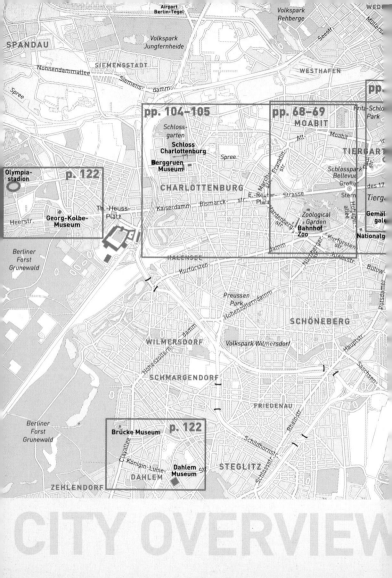

CITY OVERVIEW

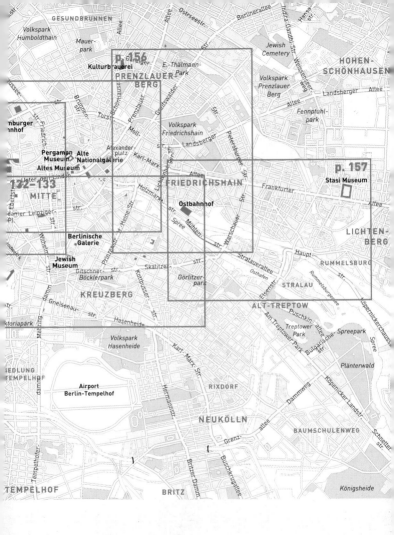

Mitte

Tiergarten

Charlottenburg

Kreuzberg

Friedrichshain and Prenzlauerberg

entertainment

planning

art glossary

index

introduction

When asked by visitors where the city centre is, Berliners like to answer: 'wherever you're standing'. That's typical of the city's independent spirit and its residents' cultivation of local identity. But for first-time visitors Berlin's fractured structure and open spaces means orientation can be difficult.

In order to simplify things, we've divided the city into five zones. **Mitte** is home to the Museumsinsel (Museum Island), once the symbol of Prussian cultural ascendancy and now a UNESCO heritage site. Mitte is also known for the best shops and restaurants and a huge number of galleries.

Tiergarten has Potsdamer Platz and the new government buildings—some of the most interesting postmodern structures in Europe—and the Kulturforum, a rich complex of museums, concert halls and libraries. And, of course, there is Tiergarten itself, Berlin's famous park.

To the west is **Charlottenburg**, with the Schloss and other important museums, as well as more upmarket shops and restaurants. Some say Charlottenburg's cultured and cosmopolitan atmosphere is Berlin at its most authentic.

Kreuzberg has two of Berlin's newest museums, the Jewish Museum and the Berlinische Galerie. Kreuzberg is where the flame of the counterculture still burns, and has a large ethnic Turkish populations as well as the city's best bars.

Prenzlauerberg and Friedrichshain are eastern districts, with significant sites like the Stasi Museum testifying to east Berlin's troubled political history. Prenzlauerberg is also special for the young and independent designers that have given Berlin a reputation as a centre for creative talent.

We hope this guide will help you get a taste for one of Europe's most interesting and varied cities. *Viel Spass in Berlin!*

MITTE

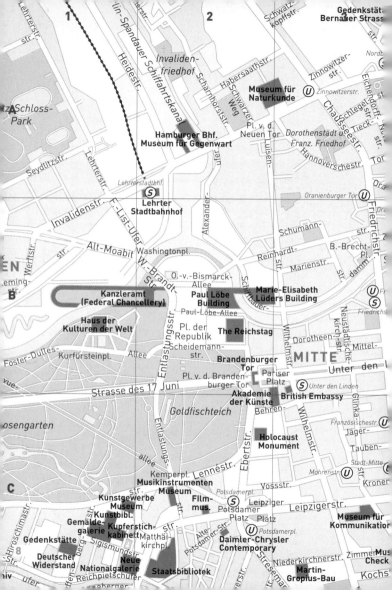

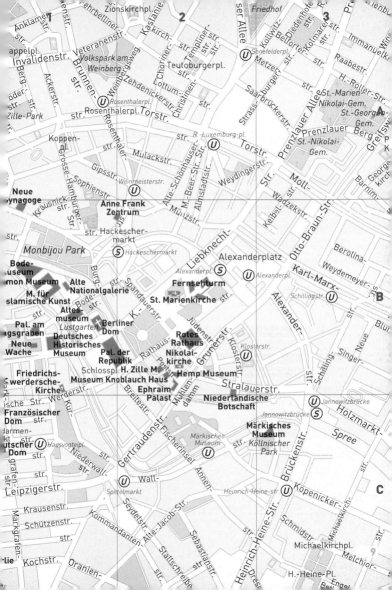

Museumsinsel

The Museumsinsel and the Collection of Classical Antiquities

PERGAMON MUSEUM AND ALTES MUSEUM

OPEN	The museums are open 10 am–6 pm, Tue–Wed and Fri–Sun, and 10 am–10 pm on Thur.
CLOSED	Mon
CHARGES	Regular admission €8, reduced €4, both include audio guide. Tickets valid for Alte Nationalgalerie, Altes Museum and Friedrichwerdesche Kirche (excluding special exhibitions). Free entry 4 hours before closing on Thur (without audio guide). No charge for children up to 16 years. Combined day ticket to all SMPK museums is €10 (reduced admission €5); three-day ticket to all SMPK museums €12 (reduced admission €6).
MAIN ENTRANCE	Museums Insel, Bodestraße 1–3 U to Alexanderplatz or S to Hackescher Markt
TELEPHONE	2090 5277
WEB	www.smb.spk-berlin.de
SERVICES	The Café Pergamon serves salads, sandwiches and basic hot dishes. A café in the Altes Museum next to the rotunda serves coffee, tea, cakes and sandwiches. Both the Altes Museum and Pergamon have shops selling books and cards.

THE MUSEUMSINSEL

The Museumsinsel (Museum Island) is the museum complex halfway down Unter den Linden, called an island because it is bordered on its eastern and northern sides by the Spree Canal. The Museumsinsel has five museums, three of which are currently open: the Altes Museum, the Pergamon Museum and the Alte Nationalgalerie. The Neues Museum and the Bode Museum are closed for renovation, and will open in 2006 and 2008.

   The collection of the Antikensammlung is split between two buildings, the Altes Museum (or 'Old Museum') and the Pergamon Museum. The Altes Museum holds the collection of minor arts

MUSEUMSINSEL

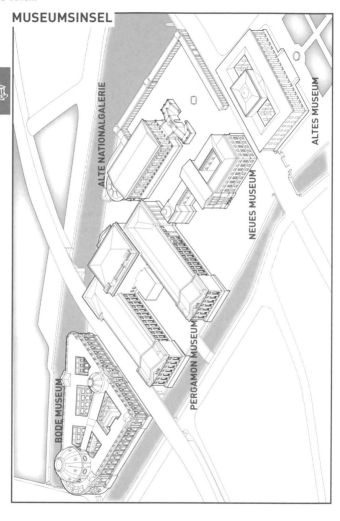

ALTE NATIONALGALERIE

ALTES MUSEUM

NEUES MUSEUM

PERGAMON MUSEUM

BODE MUSEUM

while the Pergamon holds the Collection of Classical Antiquities, the Museum of the Ancient Near East and the Museum of Islamic Art.

The seeds of the collection came from the Prussian ruling house, but after the return in 1814 of works of art stolen by French troops, Friedrich Wilhelm III decreed that the objects be brought together in a public museum. Court architect Karl Friedrich Schinkel suggested a new building on the Lustgarten opposite the Stadtschloß. Schinkel's museum (the Altes Museum) was completed in 1830. The building was designed based on the Pantheon in Rome, with a rotunda that forms the central feature of the museum's interior: both cupolas are exact half-spheres and have a circular window at their apex lighting the whole room. The rotunda is the only part of the building to have been rebuilt after World War II exactly to Schinkel's original design.

The collection continued to expand through the years, and soon it became clear that there was more art than could be shown in a single museum. In 1841 Friedrich Wilhelm IV decreed that the entire area behind the museum be developed into a district for the arts and antiquity (he also planned to have his mausoleum built there). Thus was created Museum Island. Between 1843 and 1855, the Neues Museum was constructed under August Stüler, who later also designed the adjacent Nationalgalerie. The Kaiser Friedrich Museum (now the Bode Museum) was completed on the other side of the railway track in 1912 to house the painting collection (now at the Gemäldegalerie, see p. 70).

Another gallery was required to separate the post-Classical sculpture and earlier work, and house the large architectural finds. The Pergamon Museum, named after its prize exhibit, the great Altar of Pergamon, was designed by Alfred Messel. When construction began, in 1912, the design was praised for its sober combination of Prussian Classicism with modern clarity. However, by the time it was completed, in 1930, the building's monumentality represented to many the now discredited ambition of the prewar ruling class. Plans for the interior were pared down and objects were left to 'speak for themselves', an aesthetic position known as the 'Neue Sachlichkeit' (New Objectivity).

At the end of World War II, around 70% of the complex was damaged—a fuel tanker parked outside the Altes Museum exploded and set the entire building on fire. The Altes Museum was repaired during the 1950s on the basis of Schinkel's highly detailed drawings and reopened in 1966. The exhibits, which had been stored in bunkers across Berlin, remained divided after the war. Those in the western zone came under the jurisdiction of the Preußischer Kulturbesitz and were shown in the one of the two Stüler buildings opposite the Stadtschloss in Charlottenburg. What remained of objects retrieved from the eastern zone were shown in the north wing of the Pergamon. In 1958, the Pergamon Altar, along with a number of other objects, was returned from the Soviet Union, and the Pergamon Museum fully reopened in 1959. In 1995, the two halves of the collection were reunited.

PERGAMON MUSEUM

HIGHLIGHTS

Pergamon Altar	Room I
Market Gateway from Miletus	Room III
Berlin Goddess	Gallery 2
Copies of statues by Polykleitos	Gallery 5
Statue of a girl playing knucklebones	Gallery 7
Bust of Emperor Caracalla & other emperors	Gallery 8
Ishtar Gate	Museum of the Ancient Near East

ROOM I: PERGAMON ALTAR

The **Pergamon altar** was the major find during excavations carried out at the ancient city of Pergamon on the west coast of Asia Minor (now Turkey) by Carl Humann. Pergamon had been

PERGAMON MUSEUM

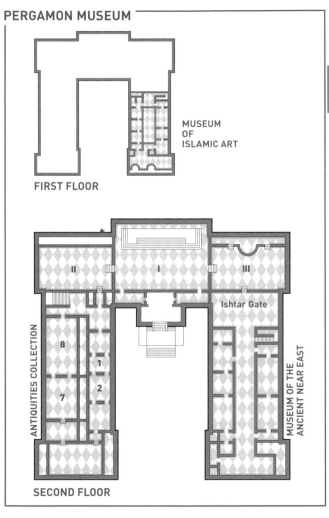

MUSEUM
OF
ISLAMIC ART

FIRST FLOOR

II

I

III

Ishtar Gate

8

1

2

7

ANTIQUITIES COLLECTION

MUSEUM OF THE
ANCIENT NEAR EAST

SECOND FLOOR

one of the major centres of the Hellenistic empire and the altar its crowning glory, described by the Roman writer Lucius Ampelius as one of the wonders of the world. Thanks to favourable terms drawn up with the Turkish authorities, the entire altar, together with the relief, was brought to Berlin. The altar was housed in a temporary building until the museum's opening in 1930.

What we see is a reconstruction of the west side of an altar built between 164–156 BC. The entire altar is likely to have been dedicated to Athene, the patron goddess of Pergamon. However, the religious significance of the altar was probably secondary to its political role as a symbol of affluence and power: it's assumed that only the royal family made sacrifices here. The occasion for the construction of the altar is thought to be the Pergamons' recent defeat of the Galileans, the barbarians alluded to in the frieze. Another theory is that it was built to affirm King Eumenes' recovery from an assassination attempt at Delphi in 172 BC. Only two words of the inscription remain: 'Queen' and 'favours'; the entire dedication may have read something like, 'King Eumenes II, son of King Attalos and Queen Appollonis, has dedicated this to the Gods in return for their favours.'

The frieze is a masterpiece of Hellenistic art, with outstanding detail and creative variation. It depicts the Gigantochamy, the battle of the gods against the giants, symbolic of the triumph of order over chaos and the Athenians' victory over the Persians, and is thought to have been created by thirty-three different master craftsmen from throughout the Hellenic world, working to an overall design by the Athenian Pyromachus. (The audio guides give a panel-by-panel account of the story of the Gigantochamy.) The altar has missing sections and originally would have been painted. The friezes on the altar itself are in their original position; the frieze on the back wall was on the opposite (east) side of the staircase, while the frieze fragments on the left and right hand walls were positioned on the north and south sides of the altar respectively. The east frieze is being restored to set right mistakes made by earlier restorations.

Up the steps, where the inner sanctum of the alter would have been situated, is a room containing fragments of a separate frieze depicting the life of Telaphus, Hercules' son and considered the founder of the city of Pergamon.

ROOM III: MARKET GATEWAY FROM MILETUS

Turning right from the main room brings you to the Roman architecture room, dominated by the **Market Gateway from Miletus**. It was built around 120 AD and destroyed by an earthquake in the Middle Ages. It was excavated by Theodor Wiegand and Hubert Knackfuß between 1903 and 1905 and brought to Berlin.

Miletus lay on the western coast of Asia Minor, around 100 km south of contemporary Izmir. Founded in the Archaic Period, under Greek occupation it was a powerful city, exporting wool and purple dye, with dependencies spread across the Mediterranean and Black Sea. Destroyed by the Persians in 494 BC, the city was rebuilt in a 'chessboard' design. Under Roman occupation the city was no longer the metropolis it had been, which had something to do with the gradual silting-up of the harbour.

The gateway was an attempt to reassert the significance of the city. It is thought that the gate was built to coincide with a visit by the emperor to Miletus in 129 BC. It combines elements of Greek and Roman styles and is typical of Roman prestige architecture. Between the columns would have stood decorative statues; notice the central 'broken pediment' at the top. Carved into the base of the gate are inscriptions by market traders to mark out their patches.

ROOM II: HELLENISTIC ARCHITECTURE

STATUE OF ATHENA (2 BC) This is a copy commissioned by King Eumenes for the Pergamon library of the gold and ivory Athens statue, which was three times as large. Eumenes had the statue made from marble mined from the Athens region, to keep as close as possible to the spirit of the original. Athena wears a helmet and breastplate: she would have held a shield in her left hand, to complete her armour. However Athena would not have inspired solely martial respect; she was also a patron of science and scholarship.

Athena is placed behind an extraordinarily delicate mosaic from the Palace of the Acropolis from the Pergamon Citadel. Notice the trompe d'oeil slip of paper bearing the artist's signature, a sign of the increasing artistic self-consciousness attached to the form.

GALLERY 1: ARCHAIC GREECE

THE BERLIN GODDESS (580–560 BC) The Berlin Goddess was acquired in 1924, and owes its excellent state of preservation to having been buried in lead casing. Not truly a goddess, but a tomb statue, she holds a pomegranate, the symbol of fertility. The original yellow and red paintwork of her robes is still perceptible on the archaic marble . The simplified main body is in contrast to the angularity of her features.

STATUE OF A YOUTH (540–530 BC) This statue stood at the oracular temple at Didyma on the west coast of Turkey. The missing arms would have extended forward to hold out a sacrificial goat or calf. Note the smile and the almond-shaped eyes, typical of sculpture of the archaic period.

Also in this room is the marble *Recumbent Lion*, which stood at a burial site south of Miletus dating back to 6 BC. It is modelled on an Egyptian sculpture; note the natural position of the lion's head and the wrinkles in the skin on the hind legs.

GALLERY 2: ARCHAIC GREECE

STATUE OF AN ENTHRONED GODDESS (460 BC) The subject is probably Persephone, goddess of the underworld. The form bridges the Archaic period and the 'severe style' of early classicism. Her arms would have been outstretched to hold a bowl in her right hand and a container for ointment or a pomegranate in her left. The form demonstrates the sculptural ideal of contraposto, the balance of relaxed and tensed elements. Drill holes in her ears and elsewhere suggest the statue was decorated.

The Votive Reliefs in this room are typical of decorations that would have adorned the burial grounds lining the roads leading into ancient Greek cities. The left-hand relief is particularly eloquent of loss, showing not the dead girl but her mourning parents; behind a housemaid puts a hand to her forehead in grief. The larger, central tombstone was typical of the memorial given to male family members. Note how these reliefs, from around 4 BC, are almost fully sculptural.

GALLERY 5: ANTIQUE COPIES OF GREEK SCULPTURE

STATUE OF A HUNTER This undated Roman copy was found in the 19th C in a villa near Rome. The subject is probably Meleäger, who, according to Ovid, slew a boar sent by Diana to cause havoc amongst ungrateful farmers. Meleäger also slew two uncles in an ensuing fight over who should take credit for the kill, and was himself slain by his vengeful mother. The distribution of weight in the pose demonstrates highly refined sculptural technique. The Greek original dates to 330–340 BC.

COPIES OF STATUES BY POLYKLEITOS Polykleitos worked around the second half of the 5th C BC, and was one of the most important Greek sculptors. His theory of relations between bodily measurements, based on the principle of contraposto, influenced sculptors up to Roman times. The technique is magnificently demonstrated in the *Torso of a Spear Bearer*, in which every individual muscle receives definition: the weight on the right leg causes the thigh muscle to bulge over the pelvis, while the right buttock is raised above the left. The right arm is relaxed, while the left, holding the spear, is tensed, causing the vein running down from the shoulder to bulge.

GALLERY 7: HELLENISTIC ART

The busts of Greek Philosophers are on your right as you enter this gallery. Plato and Socrates were firm favourites of wealthy Romans decorating their villas and gardens.

Portrait of a Ruler, Probably Attalos (early 2nd C BC), an amazingly well-preserved marble head, belonged to a full size statue that stood on the Acropolis at Pergamon. Attalos was the father of Eumenes II, who built the Pergamon altar. The portrait is both realistic and iconographic in its physiognomy—the troubled forehead, the wide eyes and the set chin mark out Attalos as a ruler (he was later deified).

METOPE DEPICTING HELIOS (3RD C BC) A *metope* is a section of stone panelling on a tomb. This one was produced around 300 BC for the Temple of Athena in Troy and is the best remaining example. Helios, the god of the sun, is shown emerging on horseback out of the sea, his halo sending out great rays of light. The impression of surging movement is created by the finely carved folds of the cloak and the diagonal representation of the team of horses.

STATUE OF A GIRL PLAYING KNUCKLEBONES This is one of numerous Roman replicas of a Greek original, made around 200 AD and discovered in Rome in 1730. (It has served as a model for many artists since.) The girl has the distinctly Roman 'melon' coiffure, as artists readily adapted Greek motives to their own tastes and purposes. It is likely the statue commemorated a dead child.

THE NUMISMATIC COLLECTION A collection of coins from Roman, Greek, Egyptian and Celtic civilisations.

GALLERY 8: ROMAN ART
THE EMPEROR CARACALLA AND BUSTS OF EMPERORS (BETWEEN 212 AND 217 AD) Caracalla was a Roman emperor of the middle Imperial Period; his sword strap and cloak indicate his military rank. He was a fearsome warrior, reputed brave enough to eat alongside lions. The other busts, each strikingly individual, include Gardianus, Constantinus and Arcadius.

SARCOPHAGUS WITH RELIEF OF THE LEGEND OF MEDEA The sarcophagus, made in Rome between 140–150 AD, depicts the four acts of Euripedes' tragedy Medea, first performed in 432 BC.

MUSEUM OF THE ANCIENT NEAR EAST

The collection provides a representative view of cultures of Sumer, Babylon, Assyria and northern Syria, ranging from prehistoric times to the Greco-Roman Period. The Museum of the Ancient Near East moved to the south wing of the Pergamon in 1926 and the collection's prize exhibits, the Ishtar Gate and Processional Way, were installed in 1930 and shown to the public in 1936. During the war unmoveable exhibits were bricked up and saved from damage.

RECONSTRUCTION OF BABYLON'S PROCESSIONAL WAY AND THE ISHTAR GATE

The gate was one of seven in the double wall surrounding Babylon, and was in fact a relatively modest piece of architecture in comparison to other monumental structures that stood in the city. The gate took its name from the nearby temple to Ishtar, the Babylonian goddess of war; the lions on the processional way were her sacred animal. The foundation inscriptions on the gate indicate it played a major role in New Year celebrations, when a procession of images of gods from throughout the land passed through.

Excavators found only countless fragments of glazed brick, through which they were able to gain an idea of the overall form of the gate and processional way. Often they were able to reconstruct whole bricks, but not all the bricks in the reconstruction are original (originals can easily be distinguished from modern copies). The animal reliefs on the gate and way would have been produced in serial fashion in moulds, but what you see here are reconstructions from original fragments.

Detail of the Ishtar Gate

The street that ran through the gate would have been around twenty metres wide and have run for two hundred and fifty metres. Only the smaller front section of the gate has been reconstructed; the model gives an impression of its full scale. Glazed brick formed the surface of the gate, which was decorated by reliefs of bulls, symbolic of the weather god Adad, and dragons, symbolic of Marduk, patron god of Babylon.

MUSEUM OF ISLAMIC ART

Located in the south wing of the Pergamon, the collection includes art of Islamic cultures from the 8th C to the 19th C, spanning a vast area from Spain to India but with a focus on the Middle East and Iran. It's lot to see if you've already walked around the antiquities collection, but very worthwhile for some beautiful examples of Islamic decorative art.

ALTES MUSEUM

HIGHLIGHTS

Rotunda with Roman copies of Greek statues

Praying Boy	14.1
Golden Fish of Vettersfeld	8.18
Busts of Caesar and Cleopatra	28.1, 28.2
Hildersheim treasure	20.12
Mosaic with a Centaur from Hadrian's Villa at Tivoli	28.3

The collection in the Altes Museum is the second half of the Antikensammlung and contains predominantly smaller scale works of Greek and Roman arts and crafts. The Etruscan terracotta collection is central to the exhibition; silverware, jewellery and votive offerings are also well represented.

The galleries are in an open plan format and are organised chronologically, thematically and geographically. There are no English labels, but the numbers in the text below correspond to the numbers on the German labels.

THE SCULPTURES OF THE ROTUNDA
The statues are Roman copies of Greek originals. They were purchased in Italy in the 18th C by Friedrich II and Friedrich Wilhelm II as decoration for their castles and gardens. Schinkel himself also made purchases for the rotunda during his trip to Italy in 1824. They were returned to their original positions in 1981 on the anniversary of Schinkel's 200th birthday.

6.5 STANDING WOMAN WITH A CHICKEN (550 BC) Statues of young women, known as *korai*, represented an ideal of female beauty. This example was found on the site of the temple of Artemis at Miletus. The gown is pleated elegantly and the shawl is

ALTES MUSEUM

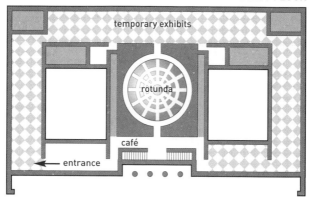

FIRST FLOOR

temporary exhibits

rotunda

café

← entrance

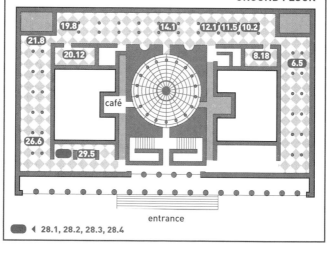

GROUND FLOOR

19.8   14.1   12.1 11.5 10.2

21.8

20.12   8.18

6.5

café

26.6

29.5

◀ 28.1, 28.2, 28.3, 28.4

entrance

a fine, clinging material, possibly Egyptian silk. She holds a chicken, a symbol of fertility. Like all statues of the archaic period, she would have been smiling.

8.18 THE FINDS FROM VETTERSFELDE The most exciting aspect of the Vettersfelde find was its geographical location, a full 1,500 km from any other recorded settlement of European Scythians.The Scythians were a nomadic tribe whom Herodotus described as invincible due to their knowledge of local terrain.

The gold fish is the most impressive of the finds. Its body is decorated with an array of animals, including an old man half man, half fish. Such worship symbols derived from the Scythians' nomadic way of life and their way of relating to the importance of animal husbandry.

10.2 RELIEF WITH ENTHRONED COUPLE (540 BC) This tomb relief shows a woman unveiling, while the man holds a drinking vessel known as a *kantharos*. The relief is laden with symbolism, from the serpent on the left-hand side, representing the underworld, to the pomegranate, the egg, the blossom and the chicken, all symbols of fertility, brought by the guests on the right. Notice the lion paws decorating the feet of the throne.

11.5 HEAD OF A BEARDED MAN (540 BC) The features of this marble head are unusual for Greek sculpture of the period. The moustache and beard are atypical and suggest an Egyptian influence; the short hair was a style worn by sportsmen or boxers; the eyes slant, again suggesting this man may not have been a native Greek.

12.1 AMPHORA SHOWING A WRESTLING MATCH (525 BC) This amphora is a good example of the many impressive vases in the collection and reflects a growing technical sophistication in vase decoration. Until the 6th C BC, figures had been painted in slip which turned black when baked; later, with the red figure technique, a transparent gloss slip was used, so that the red clay showed through, giving the images a new spatial quality. The pictures on the amphora would have had ties with historic events and been made with particular viewers in mind.

The figure to one side with the cloak and staff is probably the referee; he holds a blossom, the symbol of nobility. The other side of the amphora shows Hercules remonstrating with the priestess at the oracle at Delphi; under his arm is a tripod he has stolen in return for her refusal to give him a prophesy. You can also see the artist's inscription at the base of the vase: 'Andokides made this'.

14.1 THE PRAYING BOY (300 BC) The Praying Boy, possibly the best-known exhibit in the entire collection, is in the room behind the rotunda, on an axis with the central staircase (its original position at the museum's opening). Because of perceived homoerotic elements, the figure was thought to be Ganymede, lover of Zeus, but it is now thought to have been part of a bigger group from the temple of Helios on Rhodes, and probably depicts a worshipper. This impression is strengthened by the upturned angle of the head and the arms, which were added in France in the 17th C. The statue was first recorded in Venice in the 16th C, from it also passed through London, Vienna, Paris and Potsdam. Friedrich II reacquired it from the French and placed it outside the library window at Sanssouci.

19.8 GRAVE RELIEF OF A WARRIOR (340–330 BC) Funerals, for wealthy Greeks, were extravagant occasions, perhaps too much so for some people's taste: Cicero mentions laws passed in Athens banning gravestones which 'required more than the work of ten men over three days'. This monument shows a warrior bidding his wife farewell. In spite of the name, the tomb is probably the wife's; all figures are turned to the woman, including the child pulling at the hem of her skirt, and she is holding a garland used in funeral ceremonies.

20.12 SILVER BOWL WITH ATHENA This is one of a seventy-piece table service found in Hildesheim, around 280 km from the border of the Roman empire at the Rhine. The find was made by soldiers in 1868. Since the site lay within Prussian territory, it passed to the state collection in Berlin. Most of the set dates to the Augustan period between 27 BC and 14 AD, though the bowl itself was probably created in Alexandria in the 1st C BC. Why it was buried remains a mystery, as the service is incomplete, was created in different workshops at different times, and seems to have been owned by various people.

The inner relief of the bowl shows Athena, her robes plated gold, sitting in a rocky landscape, with her mascot, an owl, beside her. There are also beautiful motifs on the other vessels; for example, the musical instruments of the followers of Dionysus on a pair of goblets and the cupids hunting fish with a trident on a silver bowl.

21.8 PORTRAIT OF PERICLES (429 AD) Pericles was the Athenian military strategist-in-chief and a highly respected public figure with his own cult of personality—something he was keen to nurture. This is a Roman copy of a Greek original made in 429 AD that stood on the Acropolis. It would have been a complete figure, probably naked and leaning on a lance. The portrait is suitably idealised: symmetrical and emotionless, the embodiment of dignity.

26.6 STATUE OF NIKESO FROM PRIEN (280 BC) This elegant statue shows a priestess of Demeter, the goddess of fertility. The woman belonged to a wealthy family, as her draped silks testify. Her missing right arm would have been raised to carry a vessel on her head, in performance of her ceremonial duties.

28.4 HEAD OF A YOUNG ROMAN WOMAN (LATE 1ST-C BC) This is a great example of a Roman sculptor's skill in naturalistic portraiture. Produced in southern Italy, the early Imperial Period terracotta conveys an earthy, modest character.

28.1 BUST OF JULIUS CAESAR (1ST-C AD) A high degree of naturalism can be seen in this bust of Caesar in green schist, though it is thought to date from well after his death in 44 BC, when Caesar first began to be acclaimed as a great ruler.

28.2 BUST OF CLEOPATRA Cleopatra's head would have been attached to a body of the goddess Isis, in whose garb the queen liked to appear. Notice the reddish tint around her tiara: this was the base for gold plate.

28.3 MOSAIC WITH A CENTAUR FROM HADRIAN'S VILLA AT TIVOLI This mosaic is a brilliant example of the form, with an unusual degree of verisimilitude and a wide range of colours. It was created between 118 AD and 128 AD for the richly decorated villa of Emperor Hadrian at Tivoli. The mosaic was one of five similar scenes.

29.5 SARCOPHAGUS RINUCCINI Motives on this tomb from 200 AD combine legend with scenes from the life of a dead general. On the left, he can be seen holding his wife's hand in a gesture of harmony; in the central position he can be seen sacrificing a bullock in piety. On the right, the hunter Adonis is being slain by the boar sent by Mars in revenge for Adonis' affair with Aphrodite. The choice of motive acknowledges the inevitability of death and the hope of resurrection: after his death Adonis was allowed to live with Aphrodite for half the year.

Alte Nationalgalerie

OPENING TIMES	The Alte Nationalgalerie is open 10 am–6 pm, Tue–Wed and Fri–Sun, and 10 am–10 pm, Thur.
CLOSED	Mon
CHARGES	Regular admission €8, reduced €4 (both include audio guide). Ticket also valid for the Pergamon Museum, the Altes Museum (excluding special exhibitions) and Friedrichwerdesche Kirche. Free entry 4 hours before closing on Thursday (without audio guide).No charge for children up to 16 years. Combined day ticket to all SMPK museums is €10 (reduced admission €5); three-day ticket to all SMPK museums €12 (reduced admission €6).
MAIN ENTRANCE	Museumsinsel, Bodestraße
TELEPHONE	20 90 58 01
WEB	www.smb.spk-berlin.de
SERVICES	Information, tickets and cloakroom on the first floor. Toilets in the basement. There is also a museum shop in the basement that stocks a number of books in English and doubles as a café serving coffee and cakes.

HIGHLIGHTS

Frescoes from the Casa Bartholdy	Room 3.02
Karl Friedrich von Schinkel and Caspar David Friedrich	Rooms 3.05 and 3.06
Carl Blechen	Room 3.07
Cartoons by Peter Cornelius	Room 3.15
German Romans	Room 2.02
French Impressionists	Room 2.03
Max Liebermann	Room 2.13
Adolph Menzel	Rooms 1.05 to1.14
Art from the turn of 20th C	Rooms 1.15 and 1.16

The gallery is laid out more or less chronologically and begins on the third floor with the age of Goethe, around 1800. Here you find the Romantic painters, including Caspar David Friedrich and Karl Friedrich Schinkel, as well as the Biedermeier period and the Nazarenes, all of which represent the original part of the collection from the Wagener bequest. The second floor has Impressionists and the German painters (1850–1880) influenced by them. The first floor provides a contrast between the Neo-Classicism of the marbles and the realistic tendencies of the late 19th C, revolving around the Menzel collection.

THE BUILDING

In the late 18th C and first half of the 19th, Germany was made up of smaller parts, many with their own cultural centres and galleries. In 1861 it was decided that a third museum should be built on the Museuminsel, based on plans already drawn up by Emperor Wilhelm I's brother Friedrich Wilhelm IV. This would satisfy the desire of the Wilhelmine empire for a institution representing an aesthetically unified *Kulturnation*.

ALTE NATIONALGALERIE

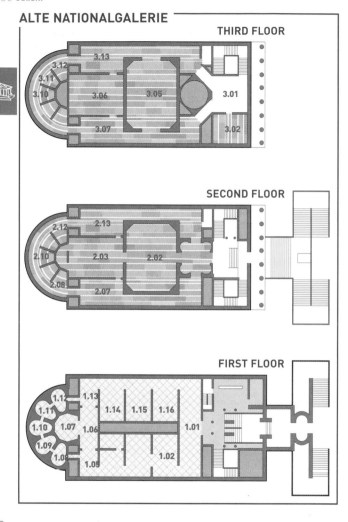

THIRD FLOOR

3.13
3.12
3.11
3.10
3.06
3.05
3.01
3.07
3.02

SECOND FLOOR

2.12
2.13
2.10
2.03
2.02
2.08
2.07

FIRST FLOOR

1.12
1.13
1.11
1.14 1.15 1.16
1.10
1.07
1.06
1.01
1.09
1.05
1.08
1.02

The gallery opened in 1876. Constructed in Nebra sandstone at the astronomical cost of three million marks, it was unlike any other European national gallery of the time, embodying both the Romantic idea of the 'aesthetic church' and the Prussian love of grandeur, with its inscription of '*Der Deutschen Kunst*' ('To German Art').

The gallery was badly damaged at the end of World War II and only provisionally restored by the East German authorities in 1955. In 1995 renovation work began on the building's exterior and in 1998 on the interior. The gallery reopened to the public as the Alte Nationalgalerie in 2001.

THE COLLECTION

The Alte Nationalgalerie holds the national collection of predominantly German art of the 19th and early 20th centuries. The basis of the collection was a bequest from banker and consul Joachim Heinrich Wagener to Prince Wilhelm I in 1861.

Max Jordan, the first director, showed a progressive spirit in acquiring works by Menzel, Böcklin and Liebermann, but patriotic spirit was high and, exasperated by historical battle scenes, genre and portrait paintings, Jordan resigned. The next director, Hugo von Tschudi, was one of the first curators internationally to purchase works by the French Impressionists. Kaiser Wilhelm II was infuriated—the inscription 'to German Art' dated to the defeat of the French in 1871—and banished Monet and the others to the third floor. When Wilhelm II decided to oversee Tschudi's purchases, Tschudi circumvented this by arranging gifts from the (primarily Jewish) bourgeoisie. Tschudi also purchased earlier works by English plein air artists such as Constable and Bonington and works by Goya, Maillol, Zorn and Segantini. But the interminable disagreements prompted Tschudi to leave Berlin for the Pinakothek in Munich, taking with him everything bought under his own initiative, including major works by Van Gogh and Gauguin.

The next director, Ludwig Justi, continued Tschudi's outward-looking policies by pushing through administrative reforms that put the gallery under parliamentary control. Justi consigned the patriotic battle-scenes to the state arsenal and replaced the sculpture hall with smaller rooms. After World War I and the demise of the Reich, Justi was able to operate a far more open acquisitions policy: works by Corinth and Slevogt and Expressionist painters from the Bauhaus generation, including Beckmann, Kirchner, Feininger and Kokoschka. Justi also bought internationally, including work from De Chirico, Modigliani, Picasso, Munch and Van Gogh. Justi was replaced in 1933 by Eberhard Hanfstaengl, whose tenure included the 'Entartete Kunst' ('Degenerate Art') exhibition of 1937, which showed works confiscated by the National Socialists from the Kronprinzenpalais.

After the war, those works that had survived in bunkers and mines in Eastern Germany were divided between the occupied areas. Works from the 19th C were returned to the Russian zone, while the Romantic paintings, the Menzel collection and the Impressionists were taken to the Allied zones of Tiergarten and Charlottenburg. The two halves of the collection remained separated until the gallery reopened in 2001.

THIRD FLOOR

ROOM 3.01–3.02 Three large-scale, neo-classical works dominate the approach to third floor galleries: **Otto Geyer**'s freeze of the *German Kulturnation*, on the stairs; **Anselm Feuerbachs**' *The Symposium* (1871–73/74); and **Gottfried Schadow**'s *Tombstone for Count Alexander von der Mark* (1788–90).

In **3.02** are frescos painted by the group of German artists painting in Rome known as the Nazarenes. The frescos were commissioned by the Prussian Consul for his palazzo, the Casa Bartholdy, and brought to Berlin on the orders of Kaiser Wilhem I in 1887. They were restored in 1960, having suffered minor war damage.

ROOM 3.05 The first of the central galleries shows Romantic paintings by polymath **Karl Friedrich Schinkel**. They play out intellectual preoccupations such as the victory of the soul over material and the drama of contemporary politics. Schinkel's cathedral paintings, modelled on Strasbourg, reflect the belief that the Gothic style grew out of the German Middle Ages, an epoch of national unity predating the Napoleonic occupation. Schinkel tempered his patriotic fervour later in life: a mellower world-view can be seen in the monumental *View of the Flower of Greece* (1825) (the original painting was lost; what we see is a copy made in 1836). In this painting, Schinkel was referring to his own project to build an 'Athens on the Spree': stylistic echoes with the columns of Schinkel's Altes Museum are clear.

ROOM 3.07 The Berliner **Carl Blechen** was one of the great talents of 19th-C German painting (Schinkel claimed Blechen was one of the best sketchers he had ever seen and Adolph Menzel was influenced by Blechen). Over a brief but productive fifteen-year career, he devoted himself to the effects of light: see the shadowy *Forest Path Near Spandau* (1834) or the glowing *Park of the Villa d'Este* (1832), painted during his stay in Italy.

Blechen was also one of first European painters to incorporate industrial motifs, as in the *Neustadt-Eberswalde Rolling Mill* (1830) or the oddly juxtaposed *Gorge Near Amalfi* (1831).

ROOM 3.06 The second of the central galleries brings you to the museum's biggest attraction: the **Caspar David Friedrich** collection. The large collection is displayed in rotation; works include his most famous painting, *Monk by the Sea* (1808–10).

Friedrich was responsible for elevating the landscape from its role as merely a backdrop for mythological and historical scenes. His famous advice to painters was to 'close your bodily eye, so you may see your picture first with your spiritual eye'. Exaggerated scenery with trademark *Rückenfigur* (figures with their backs turned) was intended to stimulate the experience of communion with God, who Friedrich believed revealed himself through nature. Yet Friedrich manages, thanks to his naturalistic handling of colour, to stay a hair away from pathos. Other notable works

Caspar David Friedrich *Der Watzman* (1824–25)

include *Abbey Among Oak Trees* (1809–10), *Morning in the Riesengebirge* (1810–11), *Der Watzmann* (1824–25; see picture above), *Solitary Tree* (1822), *Moonrise over the Sea* (1822) and *Riesengebirge* (1830–35).

ROOM 3.10–3.13 *A collection of Berlin Biedermeier*
Parade on the Opernplatz (1824–30), by **Franz Krüger**, was commissioned by the Russian Grand Duke Nicholas and returned as a gift shortly before World War I. It is interesting that the scene concentrates less on the ceremonies taking place outside the opera house and more on the socialising of bourgeois notables.

Since the early 19th C, public reading rooms had been instrumental in forming public opinion. *The Reading Room* (1843), by **Johann Peter Hasenclever**, is one of a series carried out against the backdrop of growing press censorship.

Ferdinand Waldmüller's *Prater Landscape* (1830) shows the artist's fine brushwork, typical of the tidy Biedermeier sensibility. Though the artist specialised in interiors, here he employs his technique *en plein air*.

ROOM 3.15 These cartoons by **Peter Cornelius** count among the best drawings of 19th-C Germany, and demonstrate a technique comparable to Dürer's. The cartoons were for frescoes for a never-realised Campo next to the Berliner Dom, commissioned by Friedrich Wilhelm IV. They were brought from Munich to Berlin for the opening of the Nationalgalerie in 1876.

SECOND FLOOR

On the staircase landing of the second floor galleries, look for **Rodin**'s *Man and his Thought* (1899–1900), with the kneeling artist breathing life into his creation. There is a view from the second-floor balcony over the Berliner Dom with the Palast der Republik behind.

ROOM 2.02 A major room showing the 'German Romans'. The sinister and antiheroic paintings of **Arnold Böcklin** are among the most famous images of the fin de siècle. In *Self Portrait with Death Playing the Fiddle* (1872), Böcklin was said to have added the macabre troubadour only when friends saw the painting and asked what he had been listening to. In *Honeymoon* (1878), which coincided with the occasion of his own 25th wedding anniversary, Böcklin explained why the bride looks down into the sunlit valley. Her contemplative pleasure is intruded on by her husband's flute, and though she will be seduced by him, she will never forget her own dream of paradise. *Ocean Breakers* (1879) features a naiad or a lorelei, a Rhenisch motif popular in the 19th C. Böcklin made the strings of the harp held by the nymph all the same length, 'because breakers always sound the same'. *The Isle of Death* (1883), based on the island cemetery of San Michele in Venice, is Böcklin's best-known image: it received wide circulation at the time through etched versions commissioned by the art dealer

Franz Gurlitt, and tapped into the mood of an epoch.

Hans von Marées was the most influential of the German Romans on 20th-C German artists. *The Rowers* (1873), a realistic full-size oil sketch for a fresco in Naples, plays off compositional balance against gestural freedom. In *Self Portrait with Yellow Hat* (1874), Marées flexes his stick across his knee and stares straight ahead with a look not unlike van Gogh's. Marées was living in a monastery at the time with the sculptor **Adolf von Hildebrand**, whose exquisitely poised *Youthful Man* (1881–84) is also here. Of that work, Hildebrand said that he 'wants nothing, does nothing, and simply, I do believe, exists'.

At this point, we recommend retracing your steps to rooms 2.07 and 2.08, leaving the Impressionists in room 2.03 until later.

ROOMS 2.07-2.08 These rooms show the Munich painters **Wilhelm Leibl** and **Wilhelm Trübner**, with their technically accomplished dark-tone paintings exploring texture and surface. In Leibl's *Dachau Woman and Child* (1873–74), the contours of the subjects' face and hands are minutely defined against the flat expanse of black material. Trübner's *On the Sofa* (1872) treats all surfaces with equal value, from the patterned wallpaper to the woman's face, in a mode that owes much to Courbet and the dawning of the modern style. A similar technique can be see in **Carl Schuch**'s *Still Life with Partridges and Cheese* (1885), where tone and colour, conveyed in loose and even brushstrokes, reduces the subject matter's materiality.

ROOM 2.10 Paintings by Biedermeier painter **Carl Spitzweg** include *The Poor Poet* (1839), an ironic jab at the Romantic notion of poetic melancholy. Here a stack of manuscripts lies by the stove, ready for burning, and the poet squeezes a flea between thumb and forefinger.

ROOM 2.12 *Nollendorfplatz by Night* (1925), by celebrated Jewish painter **Lesser Ury**, shows a wet Berlin night during the Weimar Republic. Ury was later included in the notorious 'Degenerate Art' (*Entartete Kunst*) exhibition of 1937.

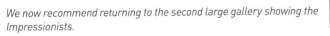

ROOM 2.13 Important paintings by **Max Liebermann** include the early dark masterpiece *Women Plucking Geese* (1872) and the contrasting light *Flax Barn at Laren* (1887). This calm, everyday scene, illuminated in the silvery Dutch light Liebermann admired so much, brings him close to the Impressionists in the next room.

We now recommend returning to the second large gallery showing the Impressionists.

ROOM 2.03 Tschudi's purchase of French Impressionists so infuriated the Kaiser that he banished them to the third floor, but they now hang where Tschudi originally planned.

The title of *Conversation* (1883) by **Edgar Degas** makes the picture unsettling—it's hard to determine whether the women are talking or huddling in silent anticipation.

In **Edouard Manet**'s *In the Conservatory* (1879), a scene of great dramatic charge and visual complexity, an older man talks softly to a woman; she stares ahead, one slack hand on her umbrella.

Auguste Renoir's *Summer* (1841), a portrait of the painter's hot and bored-looking mistress, is remarkable for its stylistic ease.

The Thinker (1881–83), a smaller version of the one at Rodin's grave, was intended to be viewed from below as part of a larger piece called 'The Gates of Hell'.

FIRST FLOOR

ROOM 1.01 This room has a selection of marble sculpture from around 1800. More of the collection, which numbers over a thousand works, is held in the Friedrichwerdesche Church. The most important artist here is **Johann Gottfried Schadow**, who at the time of *Self-Portrait* (1790–94) was sculptor to the Prussian Court. *Resting Girl* (1826) was his last work in marble; the girl's pose of appeal and withdrawal is captured in a way that combines classical and realistic elements. *Hebe* (1796) by **Antonio Canova** is a highly decorative work, demonstrating his typical inventiveness: see the cloud on which Phoebe stands.

ROOM 1.02 International landscape paintings purchased by Tschudi. *The Maypole* (c.1808–12), with its restless crowd scene, is attributed to **Francisco José Goya y Lucientes**. Its foreboding mood stands in contrast to the breezy *Higham Village on the River Stour* by **John Constable** (1804). Standing out among the landscapes is the strange *Don Quixote and Sancho Panzo* (1886) by **Honore Daumier**, best known as a caricaturist. Here he shows the emaciated knight on the left, riding away on his equally emaciated white steed, observed by his prosaic, donkey-riding servant. The landscape theme continues in **1.03** with *Spring Landscape* by **Charles-Francois Daubigny** (1862), *Seine Landscape Near Chatou* by **Jean-Baptiste-Camille Corot** (1853) and *A Square in La Roche-Guyon* (1867) by **Camille Pissarro**.

ROOMS 1.05 TO 1.14 The famously eclectic **Adolph Menzel** was a largely self-taught painter, who learned his trade in his father's lithographic workshop. We see him first in the role of court painter, with *Flute Concert of Friedrich the Great at Sanssouci* (1850–52). The Kaiser was a keen flautist, shown playing here on the occasion of a visit from his sister.

The Iron Rolling Mill (Modern Cylops) (1872–75) has the painter in social-historical mode. This painting caused a debate on the opening of the gallery in 1876 as to whether it was a legitimate subject at all. Comparing this to *Flute Concert* reveals Menzel's chameleon approach to genre.

Smaller works by Menzel include the *Balcony Room* (1845), much celebrated for its casual depiction of a half-decorated room apparently left in a hurry. With *The Artist's Foot* (1876), Menzel showed he found nothing undeserving of study.

ROOM 1.15 In this room hang paintings from the turn of the century and the Secession era, including some by **Lovis Corinth**, hailed as Germany's Impressionist. The *Family of the Painter Fritz Rumpf* (1901) is a work of flawed brilliance; the group doesn't hang together and the shadow and light is contradictory, but the painting conveys character very powerfully. *Blinded Samson* (1912), painted shortly after the artist had suffered a stroke, is an agonised statement of the human condition; in 1936 Corinth was branded as 'degenerate' for precisely this kind of existentialism.

ROOM 1.16 The exhibition ends with the period approaching World War I, on a brooding note. *Serenade* (1910), an early work by **Giorgio de Chirico**, reveals his trademark of heightened perspective and metaphysical suggestiveness. *Sin* (1912) by **Franz von Stuck** is another famous image of the fin de siècle, full of morbid carnality. Two superb paintings by **Max Beckmann** finish the floor: *Conversation* (1907), a family portrait showing the three ages of woman as observed by the artist seated in the background, and *Death Scene* (1906), where Beckmann conveys grief using a blank Expressionist style and cold, jaundiced colours.

in the area

AROUND ALEXANDERPLATZ

Fernsehturm am Alexanderplatz (TV Tower) Panorama Straße 1a, 242 33 33, www.berlinerfernsehturm.de. 9 am–1 pm, Mar–Oct; 10 am–12 am, Nov–Feb. Walter Ulbricht's baby: the colossal GDR television tower completed in 1969 (see picture on p. 42). A revolving telecafé at the top (see p. 54) provides views up to 40 km. No wheelchair access. *U* to Alexanderplatz **Map p. 9, 2B**

St Marienkirche Karl-Liebknecht Straße 8, 242 44 67, www.marien kirche-berlin.de. 10 am–6 pm, April–Oct; 10 am–4 pm, Nov–Mar. The first mention of the church was in 1294; the Gothic-Classical spire was built by Carl Langhans in 1792. Inside is the 22.6-m, 15th-C fresco *Dance of Death*, rediscovered in 1860. There is a daily tour at 2 pm and a tour of the fresco at 1 pm on Mon and Tue. *U* to Alexanderplatz **Map p. 9, 2B**

Märkisches Museum Am Köllnischen Park, 30 86 60, www.stadtmuseum.de. 10 am–6 pm, Tue–Sun. This red brick, turn-of-the-20th-century structure by Ludwig Hoffmann is now part of the Museum of Berlin History, complete with three live bears to match the heraldic symbol of Berlin. *U* to Märkisches Museum. **Map p. 9, 3C**

Niederländische Botschaft Klosterstraße 50, 20 95 60, www.dutch embassy.de. 9 am–12.30 pm, Mon–Fri. This acclaimed building, the Dutch embassy, was completed by Rem Koolhaas in 2004. *U* to Klosterstraße **Map p. 9. 2B**

The TV tower behind the Berliner Dom

Rotes Rathaus Jüdenstraße 1–9, 90 26 0. 9 am–6 pm, Mon–Fri. The city hall was built in 1869 in a neo-Renaissance style, not far from its 13th-C predecessor in the Nikolai Viertel. While Berlin was divided, the East Berlin authorities occupied the building and claimed the title 'city mayor', while the West Berlin council sat in Schöneberg. Since 1991, this has been the centre of politics for the united Berlin. *U* to Alexanderplatz **Map p. 9, 2B**

NIKOLAI VIERTEL

Located between the Rotes Rathaus and the Palast der Republik, this was the site of the eastern half of the 13th-C twin city of Cölln-Berlin (Cölln has long since melded into greater Berlin). It was reconstructed in 1987 for the 750th anniversary of the city, partly from architectural fragments and partly from imagination. It has several museums and historic buildings. U to Klosterstraße/Alexanderplatz

Ephraim Palast Poststraße 16, 24 00 21 21, www.stadtmuseum.de. 9 am–6 pm, Tue–Sun. Gallery of 17th–19th-C Berlin art in a Rococo building. **Map p. 9, 2B**

Heinrich Zille Museum Propstraße 11, 24 63 25 00, 11 am–7 pm daily. Museum of drawings by the much-loved, early-20th-C Berlin caricaturist. **Map p. 9, 2B**

Hemp Museum Mühlendamm 5, 242 48 27, www.hanfmuseum.de. 10 am–8 pm, Tue–Fri; 12 pm–8 pm, Sat–Sun. Exhibitions and info on the cultural, medical and economic value of the versatile plant. **Map p. 9, 2B**

Museum Knoblauch Haus Poststraße 16, 24 00 21 21, www.stadtmuseum.de, 10 am–6 pm, Tue–Sun. Museum of 19th-C bourgeois life in the former home of a wealthy Jewish family. **Map p. 9, 2B**

Nikolaikirche Nikolaikircheplatz, 240 020, www.stadtmuseum.de. This 15th-C church got a Neo-Gothic makeover in 1878. There is a permanent exhibition on the building's history. **Map p. 9, 2B**

AROUND HACKESCHER MARKT

Anne Frank Zentrum Rosenthaler Straße 39 (Hinterhof), 87 29 88, www.annefrank.de. 12 pm–8 pm, Tue–Sun, May–Sep; 10 am–6 pm, Tue–Sun, Oct–Apr. The Anne Frank centre has an interactive exhibition aimed at children and young adults. *U* to Rosenthaler Platz **Map p. 9, 1B**

Museum für Naturkunde Invalidenstraße 43, 20 93 85 91, www.museum.hu-berlin.de. 9.30 am–5 pm, Tue–Fri; 10 am–6 pm,

Sat–Sun. Humboldt University's natural history museum has a 22-m Brachiosaurus, the largest saurian skeleton ever mounted in a museum. *U* to Oranienburger Tor **Map p. 8, 1-2B**

Neue Synagoge – Centrum Judaicum Oranienburger Straße 28/30, 28 40 12 50, www.cjudaicum.de. 10 am–5.30 pm, Sun–Thur; 10 am–1.30 pm, Fri. The synagogue was built in 1866 in a Moorish-Byzantine style by Eduard Knoblauch. Ransacked on Kristallnacht in 1938, bombarded during the war, partly demolished in 1958, it was finally restored in 1991. It has exhibitions and an archive of Jewish life in Berlin. *U* to Oranienburger Tor **Map p. 9, 1B**

UNTER DEN LINDEN

Berliner Dom Am Lustgarten, 20 26 91 19, www.berliner-dom.de. 9 am–8 pm daily. Berlin's Neo-Baroque Protestant cathedral was built at the turn of the 20th C. Visit the tombs of the Hohenzollerns in the crypt or climb to the top of the dome. *U* to Alexanderplatz, *S* to Hackescher Markt **Map p. 9, 1B**

Bode Museum Bodestraße 1–3, 2061 6811, www.smb.spk-berlin.de. Reopening 2006, the Bodemuseum has sculpture from the early Middle Ages to the late 18th C. It also hosts the Museum for Byzantine Art and the Numismatic Collection. *U* to Alexanderplatz **Map p. 9, 1B**

British Embassy Wilhelmstraße 70-71, 20 45 70, www.britischebotschaft.de.Designed by Wilford and Partners and completed in 2000, the 9,000-m3 building has six floors and a stall for Her Majesty's horse. You can view the building by appointment. See picture on opposite page. *U* to Friedrichstraße **Map p. 8, 3B**

Deutsches Historisches Museum Unter den Linden 3, 20 30 40, www.dhm.de. 10 am–6 pm daily. Renovations to the Baroque former arsenal (Zeughaus), by Andreas Schlüter, are due to be completed in Spring 2005. The collection, which covers German history in a European context, includes technical and medical equipment, clothing and textiles, weapons and uniform, coins and medals, and posters from the former GDR. In the meantime the foyer and the new extension by I.M. Pei (2003) have changing exhibitions. *U* to Alexanderplatz **Map p. 91, B**

Friedrichswerdesche Kirche Werderscher Markt, 208 1323, www.smb.spk-berlin.de. 10 am–6 pm daily. The church, built by Karl Friedrich Schinkel, acts as an extension of the Alte Nationalgalerie, with a collection of Baroque and Romantic sculpture. *U* to Alexanderplatz **Map p. 9, 1B**

Neue Wache Unter den Linden 4. A sentry post built following designs by Friedrich Schinkel in 1818. Inside, the granite block is what remains of Hindenburg's memorial to the victims of World War I. The torch and urn containing the ashes of an unknown concentration camp victim were added by the GDR and now the monument commemorates all victims of war and tyranny throughout history. The bronze *Pietà* is by Käthe Kollwitz. *U* to Friedrichstraße **Map p. 9, 1B**

Palais am Festungsgraben Am Festungsgraben 1, 238 41 45, www.berliner-salon.de. Built in 1754 by Christian Feldmann, after the war it was used as the Soviet Union Cultural Institute. Now it is the home of the umbrella arts organisation Berliner Salon and contains the Berlin Mitte Museum, a theatre, a restaurant and artists' club, and a Tajikstani tea salon, which is well worth a visit. *U* to Friedrichstraße **Map p. 9, 1B**

Palast der Republik Unter den Linden, opposite the Berliner Dom, www.pdr.kultur-netz.de. The GDR people's palace, which opened in 1976, was left empty after reunification because of asbestos. Now cleaned out, the hall is used for exhibitions. But the Palast's days are numbered: the city planning department wants to replace it with a building whose façade will imitate the former Stadt Schloss, the Baroque palace designed by Andreas Schlüter, which originally stood on the site. *U* to Alexanderplatz, *S* to Hackescher Markt **Map p. 9, 1-2B**

The British Embassy

GENDARMENMARKT AND FRIEDRICHSTRAßE

The Gendarmenmarkt is the 17th-C square halfway up Friedrichstraße on the south side, said to be the most attractive in Berlin. The former French quarter (Huguenots moved to Berlin in 1685), it took its name from the 'Gens d'Armes' stationed there in the 18th C. It was restored during the GDR after serious war damage and renamed 'Platz der Akademie'; it got its original name back in 1990. At the centre of the square stands the Schiller Monument—removed by the Nazis and only returned to its original position in 1989. The four seated muses represent poetry (with the harp), drama (with the dagger), history (with the tablet, inscribed with the names of Goethe, Beethoven and Michelangelo), and philosophy (with the scroll, inscribed with the words 'know thyself').

Deutscher Dom am Gendarmenmarkt 202 26 90. 10 am–6 pm, Tue–Sun. Initially a modest, German Reformation church, built between 1701 and 1708; the rotunda and columned hallway were later additions under Friedrich the Great. Houses the exhibition 'Issues in German History' (in German only). See picture opposite. **Map p. 9, 1C**

Französischer Dom am Gendarmenmarkt 20 16 68 83. 9 am–7 pm daily. Built between 1701 and 1705 as a French Reformation church to serve the French Huguenot congregation. The rotunda, a later addition, houses 60 bells, under repair at the time of writing. The church contains the Huguenot museum, documenting the history of the French settlers (in German only). **Map p. 9, 1C**

Museum für Kommunikation Leipziger Straße 16, 20 29 40, www.museumsstiftung.de. 9 am–5 pm, Tue–Fri; 11 am–7 pm, Sat–Sun. This former Post building is now the museum for all things related to communication, including two of the world's rarest stamps, the famous Mauritius Penny Red and the even more famous Mauritius Twopenny Blue. The exhibition design is all about interactivity. *U* to Stadtmitte **Map p. 8, 3C**

FURTHER AFIELD

Gedenkstätte Bernauer Straße (Bernauer Straße Memorial and Berlin Wall Documentation Center) Bernauer Straße 111, 464 1030, www.berliner-mauer-dokumentationszentrum.de. 10 am–5 pm, Wed–Sun. Admission free. When the Berlin Wall went up on August 13, 1961, it divided Bernauer Straße right down the middle. What was once a 'no man's land' between east and west has now become a memorial and an archive, with exhibits on the construction of the wall and events that

The Konzert Haus (detail) and the Deutscher Dom

The World Clock

took place in Bernauer Straße. There is also an outdoor installation that tries to invoke the oppressive feeling of the wall by means of a series of concrete blocks with small slits that visitors can look through, and a sloping metal wall that corners in a dead end. The memorial is dedicated to the 'memory of the victims of communist tyranny'. The newly designed Reconciliation Chapel replaces an Evangelical church of the same name dynamited by the GDR government in 1985 to make room for more guard posts. *U* to Bernauer Straße **Map p. 8, 3A**

Mitte and Public Art from the GDR

The **World Clock** (1969) by Erich John and Hans Joachim Kunsch (see picture opposite), is the symbol of Alexanderplatz, Germany's largest—and, according to some, ugliest—square. Futuristic when it was built, it remains a popular meeting point in the otherwise disorientating space.

At the eastern side of Alexanderplatz is the Haus des Lehrers, on the site of the pre-war Teacher's Association, an unprepossessing example of international modernism with a 125-m **Socialist Realist mural** between the third and fourth floors, by Walter Womacka (1965).

The **bronze statues of Marx and Engels** on the green behind the Palast der Republik were unveiled in 1986 by Erich Hoenecker. The sculptural qualities of this memorial are limited; the grandfathers of socialism seem entirely gestureless and Marx appears to be sitting on a suitcase, implying he's ready to go. But when asked in a 1990 survey whether the monument should be removed, only a quarter of former GDR citizens said yes.

Halfway up Fridrichstraße is **Bertolt Brecht**, by the dramatist's friend Fritz Cremer (1988). The slightly smiling Brecht sits on a bench outside the Berliner Ensemble, leaving a space for a passer-by.

Women's Protest 1943 by Eva Hunzinger (c. 1980) on Rosenstraße, between Karl-Liebknecht Straße and the Hackescher Markt S-bahn station, commemorates the only protest during the Nazi dictatorship against the abduction of Jewish citizens. In 1943, in a display of strength on the home front after the defeat at Stalingrad, Goebbels ordered Jewish armaments workers in Berlin to the death camps. The German wives of the men protested outside the former Jewish Association where the men were being kept and succeeded in securing their release, albeit back into forced labour.

Israeli sculptor Micha Ullmann's **Sunken Library** (1995) on Bebelplatz, opposite the Humboldt University Law faculty and the State Opera, is on the site of the book burning of May 1933. The events are commemorated by an underground room, visible through a glass window, whose empty shelves have room for 20,000 books.

non-commercial galleries

Neuer Berliner Kunstverein (NBK) Chausseestraße 128–129. 280 70 20, www.nbk.org. 12 pm–6 pm, Tue–Fri, 2 pm–6 pm, Sat–Sun. Shows contemporary international work selected by the Berlin-based artists' collective. **U** to Oranienburger Tor **Map p. 8, 3A**

Kunstbank Brunnenstraße 188–190. 902 28 870, www.senwisskult.berlin.de. 2 pm–6 pm, Mon–Fri. Shows artists that have received grants from the Berlin Senate. **U** to Rosenthaler Platz **Map p. 9, 1A**

Kunst-Werke Auguststraße 69. 243 45 951, www.kw-berlin.de. 12 pm–8 pm, Mon–Sat. Entrance fee. The hub of the Berlin avant-garde, a four-floor gallery with temporary exhibitions of contemporary international art. **U** to Oranienburger Tor **Map p. 9, 1A**

ifa-Galerie Linienstraße 139/140. 22 67 96 16, www.ifa.de, 2 pm–7 pm, Tue–Sun. International contemporary art with focus on interculturalism. **U** to Oranienburger Tor **Map p. 8, 3A**

Deutsche Guggenheim Unter den Linden 13–15. 202 09 30, www.deutsche-guggenheim-berlin.de. 11 pm–8 pm, Mon–Wed;

11 am–10 pm, Fri, Sat, Thur. Entrance fee. Contemporary big name artists in a small, central space. *U* to Französische Straße **Map p. 9, 1B**

Sammlung Hoffmann Sophienstraße 21. 28 49 91 21, www.sophie-gips.de. Very impressive private collection of modern and contemporary art, tours by appointment on Saturdays. *U* to Weinmeisterstraße, *S* to Hackescher Markt **Map p. 9, 1A**

commercial galleries

Aedes East Rosenthaler Straße 40/41. 282 70 15, www.aedes-arc.de. 11 am–6.30 pm, Tue–Fri; 1 pm–5 pm, Sat–Sun. Contemporary artists working with architecture. *U* to Rosenthaler Platz **Map p. 9, 2B**

Alexanderplatz U-bahn Platform of the U2. Public art projects on the platform of the U2, organised by the Kreuzberg gallery Neue Gesellschaft für Bildende Kunst **Map p. 9, 2B**

Architektur Galerie Berlin Ackerstraße 19. 788 97 432, www.architekturgalerieberlin.de. 2 pm–7 pm, Tue–Fri; 12 pm–4 pm, Sat. Photography, art and installation with spatial/architectural concerns. *U* to Rosenthaler Platz **Map p. 9, 1A**

Galerie Argus Fotokunst Marienstraße 26. 283 59 01, www.argus-fotokunst.de. 2 pm–6 pm, Wed–Sun. Classic 20th-C photography, particularly narrative and documentary. *U* to Oranienburger Tor **Map p. 9, 2B**

Galerie Arndt & Partner Zimmerstraße 90-91. 280 81 23, www.arndt-partner.de. 11 am–6 pm, Tue–Sat. Experimental, contemporary art with international sweep. *U* to Kochstraße **Map p. 8, 3C**

Art & Henle Gartenstraße 9. 279 08 733, www.kunststand.de. 12 pm–8 pm, Wed–Sat. Formally and critically innovative international art. *U* to Zinnowitzer Straße **Map p. 9, 1A**

Art & Crafts Depot Gipsstraße 14. 285 70 21. 3 pm–7 pm, Wed–Fri. Old and new art from Africa. *U* to Weinmeisterstraße **Map p. 9, 2B**

Giedre Bartelt Galerie Linienstraße 161. 885 20 86, www.Giedre-Bartelt-galerie.de. 2 pm–6 pm Tue–Fri; 12 pm–6 pm, Sat. Photography from Eastern Europe and Germany. *U* to Oranienburger Tor **Map p. 9, 1A**

Contemporary Fine Arts Sophienstraße 21, 28 87 87 0, www.cfa-berlin.com. 10 am–6 pm, Mon–Fri; 11 am–6 pm, Sat. Big-name contemporary artists such as Thomas Ruff, Jürgen Teller and Gavin Turk. *S* to Hackescher Markt **Map p. 9, 1A**

Chromosome Invalidenstraße 123–124. 443 57 962, www.chromosome.de. 2 pm–7 pm, Tue–Sat. Young international contemporary art with an emphasis on media, installation and painting. *U* to Zinnowitzer Straße **Map p. 8, 3A**

Galerie Dittmar Auguststraße 22. 280 98 540, www.galerie-dittmar.de. Tue–Sat. International contemporary painting, drawing and photography. *U* or *S* to Oranienburger Straße **Map p. 9, 1A**

Galerie Deschler Berlin Auguststraße 61. 283 32 88, www.deschler-berlin.de. 1 pm–6 pm, Tue–Sat. German art from 1980 to the present. *U* to Oranienburger Straße **Map p. 9, 1A**

DNA - Die Neue Aktionsgalerie Auguststraße 20. 285 99 652, www.aktionsgalerie.de. Contemporary international art, along with music, dance and performance. *U* to Oranienburger Tor **Map p. 9, 1A**

Galerie Eigen + Art Auguststraße 26. 280 66 05, www.eigenart.com. 11 am–6 pm, Tue–Sun. Some of the big names in contemporary European painting. *U* or *S* to Oranienburger Straße **Map p. 9, 1A**

Griedervonputtkamer Sophienstraße 25. 25 29 73 07. 11 am–6 pm, Tue–Sat. Young contemporary international paintings, drawings, installations, film and videos. *U* to Weinmeisterstraße **Map p. 9, 1A**

Galerie Marianne Grob Linienstraße 115. 25 29 73 07, www.galeriemariannegrob.de. 2 pm–7 pm, Tue–Fri; 1 pm–5 pm, Sat. *U* to Oranienburger Tor **Map p. 9, 1A**

Galerie ICON Veteranen Straße 22. 443 52 420, www.galerie-icon.de. 1 pm–7 pm, Thur–Fri; 12 pm–4 pm, Sat–Sun. Contemporary painting. *U* to Rosenthaler Platz **Map p. 9, 1A**

Imago Fotokunst Auguststraße 29c. 280 45 999, www.imago-fotokunst.de. 12 pm–7 pm, Tue–Fri; 2 pm–6 pm, Sat. Old and new photography. *U* to Oranienburger Tor **Map p. 9, 1A**

Jarmuschek und Partner Spohienstraße 18. 285 99 070, www.jarmuschek.de. 2 pm–7 pm, Wed–Fri, 2 pm–7 pm; 11 am–7 pm,. Contemporary realist painting and photography. **Map p. 9, 1A**

Jüdische Galerie Berlin Oranienburger Straße 31. 282 85 29. 10 am–6 pm, Mon–Thur; 11 am–3 pm, Sun. Artists represented by the gallery. *U* to Oranienburger Tor **Map p. 9, 1B**

Galerie K + S Linienstraße 156. 283 85 096, www.galerie-k-s.de.
3 pm–7 pm, Wed–Fri; 12 pm–5 pm Sat. Shows work by artists in
residence at the Kunstlerhaus Bethanien in Kreuzberg. *U* to
Weinmeisterstraße **Map p. 9, 1A**

Mathias Kampl Auguststraße 35. 283 91 862, www.galeriekampl.de.
3 pm–8 pm, Wed and Fri; 12 pm–8 pm, Thur and Sat. Photography, works
on paper and video. *U* to Oranienburger Tor **Map p. 9, 1A**

Galerie Kapinos Gipsstraße 3. 2838 47 55, www.kapinos.de. 1 pm–7 pm,
Tue–Fri; 1 pm– 6 pm. International contemporary conceptual art. *U* to
Weinmeisterstraße **Map p. 9, 1A**

Kicken Berlin Linienstraße 155. 784 12 91, www.kicken-gallery.com.
11 am–6 pm, Tue–Fri; 2 pm–6 pm, Sat. 19th- and 20th-C photography,
including Bauhaus, Avantgarde and Neue Sachlichkeit. *U* to
Weinmeisterstraße **Map p. 9, 1A**

Klosterfelde Zimmer Straße 88–91. 283 53 05, www.klosterfelde.de.
11 am–6 pm, Tue–Sat. International contemporary conceptual art. *U* to
Kochstraße **Map p. 8, 3C**

Galerie Inga Kondeyne Hackesche Höfe, Rosenthaler Straße 40–41. 281
31 13. 2 pm–6 pm, Tue–Fri; 12 pm–5 pm, Sat. Drawings, paintings and
objects by 20th-C Berlin artists. *S* to Hackescher Markt **Map p. 9, 1B**

Kuckei + Kuckei Linienstraße 158. 883 43 54, www.kuckei-kuckei.de. 11
am–6 pm, Tue–Fri; 11 am–5 pm, Sat. International contemporary art. *U*
to Weinmeisterstraße. **Map p. 9, 1A**

Galerie.Leo.Coppi Hackesche Höf, Hof 3, Rosenthaler Straße 40–41. 283
53 31, www.galerie-leo-coppi.de, 1 pm–6.30 pm, Tue–Fri; 12 pm–6 pm,
Sat. Expressive figurative painting from the former GDR and today's
Eastern Germany. *S* to Hackescher Markt **Map p. 9, 1B**

Galerie Wolf Lieser Remise, Tucholskystraße 37. 280 98 648. 2 pm–6 pm,
Wed–Fri. Recent international contemporary art. *U* to Oranienburger Tor
Map p. 9, 1A

Müllerdechiara Weydingerstraße 10. 3903 20 40, www.müller
dechiara.com. 12 pm–7 pm, Tue–Sat. Art with a conceptual leaning, also
architectural work. *U* to Rosa Luxembourg Platz **Map p. 9, 2A**

play gallery Hannoversche Straße 1. 27 58 21 11, www.pushthebutton
play.com. 12 pm–7 pm, Mon–Sat. *U* to Oranienburger Tor **Map p. 8, 3A**

Galerie Refugium Auguststraße 19. 283 90 555, www.galerie-
refugium.de. 2 pm–7 pm, Tue–Fri; 12 pm–5 pm, Sat. Contemporary
painting, sculpture and installation with a focus on artists from Cuba. *U*
to Oranienburger Tor **Map p. 9, 1A**

Galerie Markus Richter Schröderstraße 13. 28 04 72 83, www.galeriemarkusrichter.de. 12 pm–7 pm, Tue–Sat. New minimal tendencies. *U* to Oranienburger Tor **Map p. 9, 1A**

Galerie Sandmann Linienstraße 139–140. 280 45 323, www.artsandmann.de. 2 pm–7 pm, Tue–Fri;12 pm–6 pm, Sat. Russian avant-garde art after 1950. *U* to Oranienburger Tor **Map p. 9, 1A**

Schwarzer Gegenwartskunst Schlegelstraße 31. 24 63 97 39, www.schwarzerberlin.com. 12 pm–7 pm, Tue–Sat. Young international contemporary painting, photography, video and installation. *U* to Zinnowitzer Straße **Map p. 8, 3A**

Spielhaus Morrison Galerie Rheinhardtstraße 10. 280 405 77, www.spielhaus-morrison.com. 12 pm–7 pm, Tue–Sat. Contemporary German and international painting, photography and graphics. *U* or *S* to Friedrichstraße **Map p. 8, 3B**

Glasgalerie Splinter Sophien-Gips-Höfe, Sophienstraße 20–21. 28 59 87 37, www.glasgaleriesplinter.de. 2 pm–7 pm, Tue–Fri; 11 am–4 pm, Sat. Contemporary glass along with other styles: Baroque, Biedermeier, Art Nouveau, Art Deco. *U* to Weinmeisterstraße **Map p. 9, 1A**

Galerie SPHN Koppenplatz 6. 275 94 925, www.sphn.de. 12 pm–6 pm, Tue–Sat. New painting, photography and sculpture. *U* to Weinmeister Straße **Map p. 9, 1A**

Galerie Barbara Thumm Dircksenstraße 41. 28 39 04 57, www.b.thumm. 11 am–6 pm, Tue–Fri. International contemporary art. *S* to Hackescher Markt **Map p. 9, 2B**

Völcker & Freund Galerie Auguststrasse 62. 28 09 61 15, www.voelker.de. 12 pm–7 pm, Wed–Fri; 11 am–5 pm, Sat. International contemporary art on paper and canvas. *U* to Oranienburger Tor **Map p. 9, 1A**

Galerie Wieland Ackerstraße 5. 28 38 57 51, www.galerie-wieland.de. 2 pm–7 pm, Wed–Fri; 12 pm–5 pm, Sat. Multimedia work. *U* to Rosenthaler Platz **Map p. 9, 1A**

Galerie Wohnmaschine Tucholskystraße 35. 30 87 20 15, www.wohnmaschine.com. 11 am–6 pm, Tue–Sat. International art in all genres. *U* to Oranienburger Tor **Map p. 9, 1A**

Zwinger Galerie Gipsstraße 31. 28 59 89 08. 2 pm–7 pm, Tue–Fri; 11 am–5 pm, Sat. Contemporary socially critical art. *U* to Weinmeisterstraße **Map p. 9, 1A**

eat

€   **Assel** Oranienburger Straße 21, 281 20 20 56. From 10 am, closing varies, open daily. Cellar bar/restaurant with breakfast and lunch menus of traditional German cookery. Comfy seating, a good selection of cakes and plenty of magazines make it the ideal place to come for an afternoon coffee. There's a party atmosphere on summer nights; tables on the street provides a ringside view of the city's most popular boulevard, which after dark reveals its distinctly louche character. *U* to Alexanderplatz, *S* to Hackescher Markt **Map p. 92, B**

Atame Tapas Bar Dircksenstrasse 40, 28 04 25 60, www.atame-tapasbar.de. 10.30 am–12 am, Sun–Thur; 11.30 am–1 am, Fri–Sat. Calamares, boquerones, chorizo, gambas, ensaladilla rusa...Tucked away between Hackesher Markt and Alexanderplatz, Atame passes the tapas test: it's popular with the local Spanish community. Recommended are the meat and fish tapas plates to share between two; tortilla and paella are also on the menu. Every first Sunday of the month ten courses from all regions of Spain are served up for a prix fixe €25, including an aperitif. The kitchen stays open until midnight. *U* to Alexanderplatz, *S* to Hackescher Markt **Map p. 9, 2B**

Barcomi's Deli Sophienstraße 21, 2nd courtyard, 28 59 83 63, www.barcomi.de. 9 am–10 pm, Mon–Sat; 10 am–10 pm, Sun. The Mitte branch of this popular American deli (there's also one in Kreuzberg at Bergmannstraße 21) is tucked away in a red brick hinterhof that it shares with the Contemporary Fine Arts gallery. Barcomi's specialises in coffee (from Papua New Guinea, Costa Rica, Peru, Sumatra and elsewhere) but tea drinkers won't be disappointed, with a selection including Bengal Spice, Tangerine Zinger, Emperor's Choice and Tension Tamer. The bagels are homemade and filled with a selection from the in-house deli; the all-day platters will satisfy bigger appetites. And for something sweet with your coffee? Cheesecake, carrot cake, brownies, pecan pie, all home made. Barcomi's is a great place to retreat, unwind and chat. *U* to Weinmeisterstraße, *S* to Hackescher Markt **Map p. 9, 1A**

Café Einstein Unter den Linden 42, 204 36 32. 7 am–1 am, daily. Einstein, once undisputed king of the cup of java, is now battling it out with Starbucks for the hearts of coffee-literate Berliners. Einstein takes the classic approach: wood and leather seating and staff in black and white uniform. The coffee, especially *Verlängerte* (coffee with extras), is excellent. Breakfasts, sandwiches and cakes are also available, and they keep a selection of the international press. *U* to Friedrichstraße or *S* to Unter den Linden **Map p. 8, 3B**

Hennig's Ice Cream Parlour Karl-Marx-Allee 34, 8 am–11 pm, Mon–Thur; 8 am–12 am, Sat; 8.30–11 pm, Sun. A short walk east from Alex along the Karl-Marx-Allee, past the Kino Internationale, brings you to this listed 1960s building. With its genuine GDR pleasure palace feel, Hennig's is a popular haunt, and not only in the summer: Berliners eat ice cream when there's six feet of snow on the ground. The ice cream is whipped in large steel vats behind the counters and brought out by means of metre-long spoons. Portions range from the 90-cent cup to the €9 bucket. *U* to Schilling Straße, *S* to Alexanderplatz **Map p. 9, 3B**

Kuchi Gipsstraße 3, 28 38 66 22, www.kuchi.de. 12 pm–12 am, Mon–Thur; 12.30 pm–12 am, Fri–Sun. Well-placed sushi bar in the heartland of the art mile, just off Auguststrasse. It's hip and relaxed with some eye-catching, ancient-meets-modern interior design. Good for a snack, with seats inside or in the yard. Very popular, especially at weekends; if you want dinner, it's a good idea to book ahead. *U* to Weinmeisterstraße, *S* to Oranienburger Straße **Map p. 9, 1A**

Kurhaus Alte Schönhauser Straße 35, 24 63 25 23. 10 am–10 pm, Mon–Fri; 11 am–4pm, Sat. The emphasis in this bistro is on healthy eating, with warm vegetarian food, sandwiches and wide selection of freshly squeezed fruit juices. A great place to come for a light lunchtime vitamin-booster when doing Mitte. It's cheap and lively with an informal, back-room feel; the café is a mini gallery and does a sideline in music by local techno artists. *U* to Weinmeisterstraße **Map p. 9, 2A**

Telecafé Panoramastraße 1a, 242 33 33, www.berlinerfernseh turm.de. 10 am–12 am, daily. The restaurant at the top of the television tower rotates twice each hour, offering lunch, coffee and cakes, and views up to 40 km. Unless you book, plan on queuing a while for the privilege, especially at weekends. It's unbeatable for a romantic dinner, with the lights of Berlin twinkling 207 m below; if you feel a twinge of vertigo, nerve-settling muzak is provided. **U** or **S** to Alexanderplatz **Map p. 9, 2B**

Monsieur Vuong Alte Schönhauser Straße 46, 87 26 43, www.monsieurvuong.de. 12 pm–12 am, Mon–Sat; 2 pm–12 am, Sun. Excellent Vietnamese cooking has made this one of the most visited restaurants in Mitte, which makes finding a seat tricky (you can't book). They also do an energy fruit shake: good shopping fuel. **U** to Weinmeisterstraße **Map p. 9, 2A**

€€ **Französische Hofs** Jägerstraße 56, 20 17 71 70. Open from 11 am, kitchen open until 12 pm. Lunch menu 11 am–3 pm, Mon–Fri. This restaurant offers a view of the Gendarmenmarkt, perhaps Berlin's most picturesque spot. A great place for lunch: get a place in the sun and watch sharp types from business, media and politics weave through phalanxes of retired German Kultur tourists. The menu is the ubiquitous 'International German Cuisine', though it's reasonably priced considering the location. **U** to Hausevogteiplatz or Französische Straße **Map p. 9, 2B**

Galeries Lafayette Französische Straße 23, 2 09 48 0. 10 am–10 pm, Mon–Sat. Berlin has a strong French tradition through the immigration of the Huguenots in the 18th C, and much of its slang still contains Francophone derivations (like 'es ist alle', meaning 'it's run out', from the French shopkeepers' cry 'C'est allez'). The Galeries Lafayette, the French food hall near the Gedarmenmarkt, continues the tradition. 'Gal Laf' combines a patisserie, wine shop, charcuterie, fishmonger's, cheese shop, bistro, café, épicerie, bookshop and kitchenware shop. Come to shop and eat: with a selection covering everything from terrine of venison to chocolate éclairs, it's the place to come. **U** to Französische Straße **Map p. 9, 1C**

Hackescher Hof Rosenthaler Straße 40/41, 283 52 93, www.hackescher-hof.de. 9 am–1 am, Mon–Fri; 9 am–2.30 am, Sat–Sun. These expansive rooms at the hub of the 'Neue Berlin' serve food any time you want it. The set menu ranges from the club sandwich to the Wienerschnitzel, and cakes and tarts baked by the in-house Konditorei. Though not the cheapest option in town, the Hackescher Hof is uniquely well-placed and beloved by tourists, though without being tacky. **U** to Weinmeisterstraße, **S** to Hackescher Markt **Map p. 9, 2B**

Kasbah Gipsstraße 2, 27 59 43 61, www.kasbah-berlin.de. 4 pm–12 am, Tue–Sun. Highly regarded Moroccan restaurant,

Galeries Lafayette

specialising in pastilla (chicken, almonds, parsley and coriander wrapped in thin pastry) and Tajine (a Maghrebi mix of sweetly spiced meat, fruit and vegetables, served with couscous or semolina). Vegetarians will find almost nothing to eat. *U* or *S* to Oranienburger Tor **Map p. 9, 1A**

Kellerrestaurant in Brecht-Haus Chauseestraße 125, 282 38 43. Kitchen from 6 pm–11 pm daily. Bertolt Brecht and his wife Helene Wiegel moved to the first floor of Chauseestraße 125 in 1953; the former cellar of the house (the Brecht Archive) now has a small restaurant. During the years of wartime exile Brecht longed for home cooking, and Wiegel made a virtue out of the necessity of making do. The kitchen today honours her skills with a variety of goulashes, schnitzels and roasts, as well as the speciality of the house, the Tafelspitze: bouillon of beef in a sweet schnapps sauce. The restaurant, decorated with original stage memorabilia and photographs, is wonderfully *gemütlich* on a cold winter's night. In warm weather food is served in the courtyard. *U* or *S* to Oranienburger Tor **Map p. 8, 3A**

Mirchi Oranienburger Straße 50, 28 44 44 82, www.mirchi.de. 12 pm–1 am, Sun–Thur;12 pm–2 am Fri, Sat. This impeccably run restaurant at the western end of the Straße serves a Singaporean cuisine—a mixture of Tamil, Chinese and Malay, with delicate and juicy curries. *U* to Oranienburger Tor, *S* to Oranienburger Straße **Map p. 8, 3A**

Sophieneck Große Hamburger Straße 37, 28 34 065, www.sophieneck-berlin.de. 11 am–1 am, Sun–Thur; 11 am–2 am, Fri–Sat. Highly recommended for a family meal: wood-panelled, comfortable and friendly. This is a place where you can spend the good part of five hours—you need at least that to digest. If you're keen on *deftige* (strong-flavoured) German cooking then the *Schweinhaxe* (leg of pork) is for you. If you're squeamish about lots of wobbly fat then try one of the North Sea herring dishes. *S* to Hackescher Markt **Map p. 9, 1A**

Wein Guy Luisenstraße 19, 28 09 84 84. 7 am–11.30 pm daily, breakfast from 7 am, lunch menu 12 pm–3.30 pm; dinner menu after 5 pm. This large and roomy restaurant and wine bar is near the Charitée, the central hospital. The cooking is German: there's a breakfast buffet from 7 am, a two-course business lunch from 12 pm and an evening menu from 5 pm. The cellar holds 600 wines— tastings can be arranged. The Bundestag supplies Guy's with a regular clientele; the large tables make it popular for media get-togethers. A good option for a smart meal without spending too much. *U* or *S* to Friedrichstraße **Map p. 9, 3B**

Zwölf Apostel, Georgenstraße 2, 201 02 22, www.12-apostel.de. 12 pm–12 am Sun–Thur; 12 pm–1 am Fri–Sat. John, Simon, Paul, even Judas: they're all pizzas. It's the last supper every night of the week at the Twelve Apostles, a Berlin institution under the arches of the S-Bahn. Popular by day with students of the Humboldt—pizzas are only €5.95 between 12 pm and 4 pm, Mon–Fri—at night it's busy with an after-work crowd. You can come here just to drink, too, but when you see those thin-crust pizzas being ferried through the cavernous interior it's hard to resist the temptation. *U* or *S* to Friedrichstraße **Map p. 9, 1B**

€€€Borchardt Französische Straße 47, 203 87 110. 12 pm–12 am daily. Calf's liver in calvados sauce, roast leg of venison, entrecôte with sauce Béarnaise...This is top end, modern French cuisine, with a menu that changes daily. There's been a a restaurant here since 1853 and the original tiled floor and pillars give the large room a stately, turn-of-the-20th-century feel. A courtyard opens during the summer. It's popular with politicians and other movers and shakers, so book a table. *U* to Französische Straße **Map p. 9, 1C**

Al Contadino Sotto la Stelle August Straße 34, 030 281 9023, www.alcontadino.com. Open from 6 pm, closing time varies. 'The Farmer under the Stars' is ideal for a romantic evening. The owners get their ingredients delivered direct from their homeland in Basilicata, a region in southern Italy that subsists entirely on agriculture and is renowned for its cheeses, fruit and vegetables. Unassuming to the point of keeping the red-chequered tablecloths, Al Contadino serves the best Italian food in Mitte. *U* to Weinmeisterstraße **Map p. 9, 1A**

BARS

Café Burger Torstraße 60, 28 04 64 95, www.kaffeebuerger.de. From 7 pm, Sun–Thur; from 8 pm, Fri–Sat. This bar/club is the home of the cult party night 'Russen Disko', founded by Russian émigré author Vladimir Kaminer. During the DDR the venue was the haunt of actors from the nearby Völksbühne; the old room retains the original wallpaper and furnishings. Owner and well-known poet Bert Papenfuss keeps up the bohemian tradition with readings and performances. Very popular with a diverse clientele, from parties of Ukrainian au pairs out on the tiles to fringed aficionados of the Neue Deutsche Welle. *U* to Rosa Luxemburg Platz **Map p. 9, 2A**

Deponie Georgenstraße 5, 201 65 740, www.deponie.de.
9 am–12 am Mon–Fri; 9 am–1 am, Sat–Sun. A straightforward pub
with good beers and an interesting line in décor—one of the rooms
has a horse-drawn carriage hanging from the ceiling. *U* to
Friedrichstraße **Map p. 9, 1B**

Gorky Park Weinbergsweg 25, 448 72 86. 6 pm onwards, daily. A
Russian café-bar at the bottom of Weinbergsweg, the road up to
Prenzlauerberg, it's the little brother of the posher Pasternak on
Knaackstraße. The small but good and moderately priced menu
has blinis, borscht and *solyanka*—but don't count on getting a table
if you haven't booked, Gorky Park gets packed in the evenings. In
the summer the tables spill out onto the pavement, in the winter
the drinkers squeeze in under the portraits of Pushkin. *U* to
Rosenthaler Platz **Map p. 9, 1A**

keyser sozé Corner of Tucholskstraße/Auguststraße, 28 59 94 89. 9
am–3 am daily. A restaurant-cum-bar at a main junction of the
Auguststraße, serving all-day breakfast, plus lunch from 11.30
am–4.30 pm and dinner from 6 pm. Drink a *milchkaffee* and watch
the street life. Later the joint gets busy, especially when there's
been an opening night at the Kunst Werk gallery a few doors down.
U Oranienburger Tor, *S* to Oranienburger Straße **Map p. 9, 1A**

Newton Charlottenstraße 57, 20 29 54 21, www.newton-bar.de.
10 am–3 am, Sun–Thur; 10 am–4 am, Fri–Sat. Named after
photographer Helmut Newton, with ox-blood leather seats, life-
size photographs of nude glamour models, a whisky list the length
of a novella, and a humidor—everything man could want, surely.
They've even named a cocktail the 'Sumo' after a photo series: it's
a two-person affair containing vodka and triple sec and weighing in
at €20. No, the Newton isn't cheap, but it's one of the slickest
joints in town if you feel like a malt and a thick cigar. *U* to
Stadtmitte **Map p. 9, 1C**

Reingold Novalisstraße 11, 28 38 76 76, www.reingold.de. Open
from 7 pm onwards, daily. Reingold has a long bar, lots of comfy
seating, low lighting and one of the most comprehensive cocktail
menus in town. Popular with a smart, well-heeled crowd; the
barmen were recently voted Berlin's coolest. A good place to come
for a pre-dinner sour or post-dinner fruity drink. DJs most
evenings. *U* or *S* to Oranienburger Tor **Map p. 8, 3A**

Ständige Vertretung (StäV) Schiffbauerdamm 8, 030 282 39 65,
www.staendigevertretung.de. 10 am–1 am daily; kitchen
11 am–12.30. The Ständige Vertretung was what the Federal Republic

of Germany called its unofficial embassy in East Berlin: not an inch of wallpaper shows through the collection of political memorabilia. The StäV caters to politicians, journalists, theatre-goers and tourists. The menu includes '*Himmel und Ääde*' (heaven and earth—blood sausage with mashed potato and apple), *Rheinische Sauerbraten* (marinated beef) and *Flammkuchen* (pancake), to be washed down by one of the wide selection of Rhenish wines or a Kolsch (Cologne beer). Gerhard Schroeder has commended the StäV for its contribution to good relations between the old and the new capitals. *Prost!* **U** or **S** to Friedrichstraße **Map p. 8, 3A**

Café Zapata (at the Tacheles building) Oranienburger Straße 54, 282 61 85, super.tacheles.de. To talk '*tacheles*' means to talk frankly. A shopping arcade in the 1920s, Tacheles became a famous squat in the1990s and still operates as a studio complex for visiting artists in residence. Tacheles has so far warded off interested developers and retained its alternative identity. It's a popular drinking hole for travellers and backpackers, who can sit out back in the sculpture garden, or inside in the grungy interior. Live bands on stage most evenings; the High End 54 cinema is upstairs. **U** to Oranienburger Tor **Map p. 8, 3A**

White Trash Torstraße 201, 0179 473 2639, www.whitetrash fastfood.com. From 6 pm onwards, Tu–Sun. This former Chinese-restaurant-turned-bar is an institution among the international art-punk crowd. They've not bothered to redecorate and the interior resembles a psychedelic Shanghai brothel. For their cocktails and long drinks they give you a choice between 'Top Shelf' and 'No-Name' ingredients, while the kitchen serves salads, soups, burgers and barbequed steaks (there are also some vegetarian options) and desserts, all for under €10. There are club nights here too, which get wild, and on weekends you pay a minimal entrance fee. **U** to Oranienburger Tor **Map p. 9, 1A**

Windhorst Dorotheenstraße 65, 20 45 00 70. From 6 pm, Mon–Fri; from 9 pm, Sat–Sun. The Windhorst is a small bar with a big reputation. The drink specials tend towards the sour: Laurel's Punch, with passion fruit and rum, or the Forgotten Letter, with limette, cranberry, and gin. The US embassy is next door and staff from the nearby ZDF (central TV) like to drop in, as well as Brits from the Berlin School of English. The open-ended opening hours means it stays open until around 2 am in the summer and 3 am or 4 am in the winter. **U** or **S** to Friedrichstraße **Map p. 8, 3B**

shop

CLOTHES

Fiona Bennett Große Hamburger Straße 25, 280 96 330, www.fionabennett.com. 10 am–6 pm, Mon–Fri; 12 pm–6 pm, Sat. These designs, by a hat designer of worldwide repute, have style and humour in equal measure. Two rooms, the first with cocktail hats, including the feathered 'Cabaret' cap, the mauve sea anemone, or even the stiletto, and a second room for daytime hats with wide brims and 1920s references. All the hats are made in the studio at the back, and can be ordered to fit. If you visit only one shop in Mitte, this should be it! **S** to Hackescher Markt **Map p. 9, 1A**

Laufstieg Jägerstraße 61, 65 47 01 78. 10 am–8 pm, Mon–Sat. A women's boutique with international labels, including Ivan Grundahl from Copenhagen, Lilith from Paris and Annett Röstel from Berlin. The clothes are aimed at the professional woman looking for individual styles with close attention to detail. Annette Röstel in particular is a label to look out for: striking silhouettes and interesting combinations of materials and textures, including felt, leather and Japanese fabrics. **U** to Französische Straße **Map p. 8, 3C**

Andreas Murkudis Münzstraße 21 (Hinterhof), 308 819 45. 12 pm–10 pm, Mon–Fri; 12 pm–6 pm, Sat. Worth a visit for the shop itself, which is really more of a gallery, set back from the street in the attractive old court. Now with two spaces, the larger for big-name labels, accessories and product design, the second smaller space for changing collections, specialising in Berlin designers. Look out for Frank Leder, who uses original 1930s and 1940s buttons and trimmings in a modern-meets-classic men's wear range, as well as Pulver for smart modern clothing for women. A must for anyone interested in what's happening in top-end, cutting-edge fashion in Berlin. *S* to Hackescher Markt, *U* to Alexanderplatz **Map p. 9, 2B**

Quartier 206 Friedrichstraße 71, 20 94 62 40, www.quartier206.com. 10 am–10 pm, Mon–Fri; 10 am–6 pm, Sat. Gucci, Cerruti, YSL, Moschino, Louis Vuitton, et al. In fact, haute couture does not sit as easily in Berlin as it does in Munich or Düsseldorf, cities with far more self-assurance (not to mention wealth). The Lutter and Wegener café and wine bar on the lower floor does its best to keep up with the Joneses, serving champagne and oysters for €7. So sink back in one of the leather chairs and observe the denizens of posh boutiques stalking around like members of a threatened species. *U* to Französische Straße **Map p. 8, 3C**

Villa Caprice Dircksenstraße 37, 48 48 68 98, www.villa-caprice.de. 12 pm–12 am, Mon–Thur; open from 12 pm onwards Fri–Sat. An outlet for designer objects on the ground floor; funky, girly women's clothing in the basement; and a café at the front. You can socialise with other customers and not be pressured to buy anything. Coffee is served with Smarties, which ought to tip the balance for you. *U* to Alexanderplatz, *S* to Hackesher Markt **Map p. 9, 2B**

SHOES

Barfuss oder Lackschuh Oranienburger Straße 89, 28 39 19 91, www.massschuhe.net. 12 pm–6.30, Mon–Fri; 11 am–3 pm, Sat. Oldest shoe shop on the Hackescher Markt, specialising in designers from Italy and Spain. As the name ('barefoot or patent leather') suggests, the selection has something for every occasion, from wooden-soled sandals to sexy heels. For men, there are some unusual shapes, the kind only the Italians can do right. *U* to Alexanderplatz, *S* to Hackesher Markt **Map p. 9, 1B**

Ricardo Cartillone Dircksenstraße 48/Oranienburger Straße 85/Savignyplatz 4/5, 28 04 07 11, www.ricardocartillone.com. Ricardo Cartillone introduced the pointy shoe to Dresden and Jena. Styles for men tend towards natty understatement, while for women there is a range from strappy sandals through to knee-length boots. *U* to Alexanderplatz, *S* to Hackesher Markt **Map p. 9, 2B**

Trippen Factory Outlet Chauseestraße 35, 2nd courtyard on the left, 3rd floor, 28 04 933, www.trippen.com. 1U am–6 pm, Mon–Fri. A Berliner success story: ten-year-old shoe label Trippen has a

flagship store in the Hackesche Hof IV, a gallery at Alte
Schonhauser Straße 45, and a display space for the current
collection and rareties in Knaackstrasse 26, as well as three stores
in Japan. This outlet in the red brick factory buildings at the
northern end of Mitte offers discounts on overstock and shoes with
small faults. Trippen's designs combine combine a casual and
formal look in original silhouettes; all shoes are handmade from
natural leather and intended for durability. Their range includes
clogs with colourful leather straps combining 1970s styles and
Japanese economy of form, and the 'cups', an ergonomic shoe
made made by molding leather to create a 'footshell'. Your feet will
thank you for a visit! *U* to Zinnowitzer Straße **Map p. 8, 3B**

BOOKS AND MUSIC

Kultur Kaufhaus Friedrichstraße 90, 030 2025 11 11, www.dussmann.de.
10 am–10 pm, Mon–Sat. The 'Culture Department Store' is owned
by the worldwide Dussmann group. This three-storey store is
excellent for music of all genres, but especially classical, which
has the basement to itself. There is also a very good international
travel book section and a respectable English language section.
There is internet access on the 2nd floor. Also has a small café and
customer toilets. *S* or *U* to Friedrichstraße **Map p. 8, 3B**

Pro qm Alte Schönhauser Straße 48, 247 285 20, www.pro-qm.de.
12 pm–10 pm, Mon–Fri; 11 am–4 pm, Sat. Bookshop specialising in
architecture, design, photography, cultural theory and an
exhaustive selection of independent magazines. At least half the
stock is in English. Highly recommended. They also run a lecture
series and host events. (The walls of the shop have the original
tiling from around 1880.) *U* to Weinmeisterstaße **Map p. 9, 2A**

Neurotitan, Schwarzenberg e.V Rosenthaler Str. 39, 308 725 76,
www.neurotitan. Art gallery, clothes shop, indie bookshop and
second-hand record store, Neurotitan is a trash-lover's paradise.
The shop belongs to Schwarzenberg e.V, the umbrella assocation
that occupies the building and works in the media, arts, cultural
history and with youth. *U* to Weinmeisterstaße **Map p. 9, 2A**

Smart Travelling Münzstraße 21 (Hinterhof), 280 936 99, www.smart-
travelling.net. Although 'Smart Travelling' is an online,
subscription-only travel guide to all the major cities in Europe, all
the destinations can be browsed free of charge at the shop, which

also has a selection of products from the cities it covers. Call it tourism with Berliner know-how. *S* to Hackescher Markt or *U* to Weinmeisterstaße **Map p. 9, 2A**

ACCESSORIES AND INTERIOR DESIGN

Dom Friedrichstraße 76, 20 94 73 95, www.dom-ck.com. 11 am–10 pm, Mon–Sat. Dom is an international chain with outlets in Amsterdam, Paris and New York. This shop in the underground arcade of the Quartier 205 is a treasure-trove of retro-style interior design, ranging from amusingly tacky and affordable accessories to more serious lounge-lizard furnishings. Brian Eno fans will appreciate the inflatable chill-out room, shaped like a mini Epcot centre, at €299. *U* to Französische Straße **Map p. 8, 3C**

Indigo Dircksenstraße 50, 28 09 68 92. 11 am–10 pm, Mon–Fri. Silk saris in exquisite colours, as well as hand-printed bedclothes, tablecloths, shawls and a selection of jewellry in lapis, amber and silver. Downstairs there's wooden furniture from Indonesia. *U* to Alexanderplatz, *S* to Hackesher Markt **Map p. 9, 2B**

Milk Berlin Almstadtstraße 5, 246 30 867, www.milkberlin.com. 2 pm–7 pm, Mon–Fri. Bags are big in Berlin! This cult designer specialises in bright, practical, hand-made (and therefore not cheap) bags. Sizes range from the washbag to the beachbag. Great for enthusiasts looking for something unique to the city. *S* to Hackescher Markt, *U* to Alexanderplatz **Map p. 9, 2B**

re-store Auguststraße 3, 28 09 58 42, www.re-store.de. 11 am–10 pm, Tu–Fri; 10 am–4 pm, Sat. This basement shop is not a straightforward retailer but more of a work in progress, with a clubby atmosphere where customers can sit around and discuss the design philosophy with the owners. The basic form is the cube, which is used in units of varying uses and sizes. The adaptability of the furniture is a response to the mobility of the modern Berliner, who may exchange flats on a yearly basis: a filing cabinet may become a coffee table in another context. The shop is also a showroom for other Berlin designers: Flip Sellin, for example, who make 'modular sofas'. But it's not all stern geometry: the range of kids' toys and fashions add colour and chaos to the mix. *U* to Oranienburger Tor **Map p. 9, 1A**

Schönhauser Neue Schönhauser Straße 17, 281 17 04, www.schoenhauser-design.de. 12 pm–10 pm, Mon–Fri; 11 am–6 pm, Sat. Get your 1970s KLM airline bag here!

Kitchenware, clothes, beachwear, toys, jewellry, wallpaper, all inspiringly buyable. The back room has antique furniture from the GDR: low, rectilinear sofas and hanging lamps that look like works of kinetic art give the showroom the feel of a Godard film set. There's another shop in the yard with contemporary designs. Schönhauser combines affordable modern imitation with authentic Ost retro, and is one of Mitte's biggest draws. Don't miss it! *U* to Weinmeisterstraße **Map p. 9, 2A**

Waahnisinn Berlin Rosenthaler Straße 17, 030 282 00 29. Second-hand clothing shop used by the film industry for costumes and props. Retro furniture, fittings, jewellery and clothing: from worn jeans to 1920s sequined dresses, from the Weimar Republic look to the Marlon Brando. Also does a line in unusual items of furniture such as the dentist's reclining chair, should you be looking for one. *U* to Rosenthaler Platz **Map p. 9, 2A**

GIFTS

Ampelmann Hackesche Hof, 44 04 88 09. It may be hard to believe, but the little man you see on traffic lights in the eastern half of the city (a leftover from the GDR) has prompted the creation of this shop. It sells all manner of products featuring the quaint little fellow. Bottle openers, vases, ice moulds, candles, bookends, key rings, corkscrews... The reason he's so chubby is that he maximises visibility. **Map p. 9, 2B**

Original Erzgebirgekunst Sophienstrasse 9, 282 67 54. 11 am–7 pm, Mon–Fri; 10 am–6 pm, Sat. The milk maid, the goatherd, the traveller, the hunter, the lord mayor...put a little cone of incense in their chests and they'll puff away contentedly for hours: Räuchermännchen hark back to a world where everyone knew his place. They are made in the Erzgebirge mountains on the Czech–German border. **Map p. 9, 1A**

Metamorph Oranienburger Straße 46/47, 40 04 460, www.maskworld.com. 11 am–11 pm, Mon–Sat. The scariest masks on the market: lightweight and alarmingly lifelike, since the foam latex 'second skin' follows the wearer's own facial expressions. The shop on Oranienburger Straße shows a selection of models, ranging from the Sci Fi (shark man, cyborg), through to Fantasy (orcs, ogres and golems) and Horror (Hannibal and the Mummy) to the almost-normal (the butcher, the terrorist, the monk) and personalities (Lenin, Reagan, Helmut Kohl). *U* to Oranienburger Tor **Map p. 9, 1A**

MARKETS

Flohmarkt an der Museumsinsel am Zeughaus und Kupfergraben, 0172 301 88 73, 11 am–5 pm, Sat–Sun. Market on the tourist route specialising in products from Eastern Europe. *U* to Friedrichstraße **Map p. 9, 1B**

The Neptune Fountain

TIERGARTEN

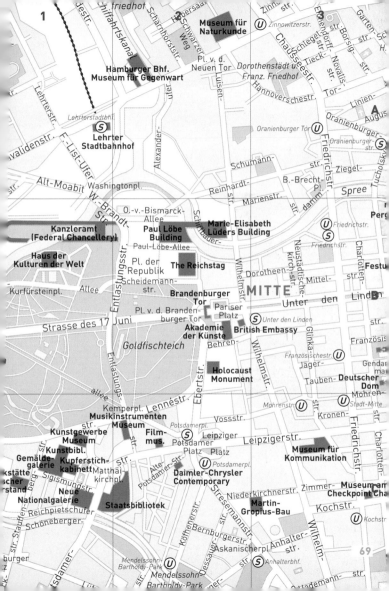

1

Jestr.

Schiffahrtskanal

friedhof

Scharnhorststr.

Ebersaal

Schwarzer Weg

Museum für Naturkunde

Zinnwitzerstr. Ⓤ *Zinnowitzerstr.*

Invalidenstr.

Elsenstr.

Chausseestr.

Schlegel- Borsig-

Garten-

Tieck-

Novalis-

str.

str.

str.

Hamburger Bhf. Museum für Gegenwart

Pl. v. d. Neuen Tor

Dorothenstädt. Franz. Friedhof

Lüsen-

Hannoverschestr.

Tor-

str.

Linien-

Augus

A

Lehrterstr.

Lehrterstadtbhf.

Ⓢ

Lehrter Stadtbahnhof

Oranienburger Tor Ⓤ

Oranienburger

str.

Friedrichstr.

Oranienburger str.

Ⓢ

Tuchol-

Invalidenstr.

Alt-Moabit

F-List-Ufer

Washingtonpl.

W.-Brandt-Str.

Alexander-

ufer

Schumann-

str.

B.-Brecht-Pl.

Ziegel-

Spree

Reinhardt-

Marienstr.

str.

damm-

Perg

O.-v.-Bismarck-Allee

Kanzleramt (Federal Chancellery)

Paul Löbe Building

Paul-Löbe-Allee

Marie-Elisabeth Lüders Building

Scheidebauer-

Ⓤ *Friedrichstr.*

Ⓢ

Friedrichstr.

Charlotten-

Haus der Kulturen der Welt

Entlastungsstr.

Pl. der Republik

The Reichstag

Dorotheen-

str.

Neustädtische-

kirch-str.

Mittel-

MITTE

str.

Festu

Kurfürsteinpl.

Allee

Scheidemann-str.

Brandenburger Tor

Pl. v. d. Branden- burger Tor

Pariser Platz

Unter

den

Linden

B

str.

Strasse des 17 Juni

Entlastungs-

Goldfischteich

Behren-

Akademie der Künste

Ⓢ Unter den Linden

British Embassy

Glinka-

Französis

allee

Wilhelmstr.

Französischestr.

Ⓤ

Jäger-

Gendar

ma

Holocaust Monument

Ebertstr.

Tauben-

Deutscher Dom

Kemperpl. Lennéstr.

Mohrenstr. Ⓤ

str.

Mohren-

Ⓤ Stadt-Mitte

Musikinstrumenten Museum

Vossstr.

Kronen-

Friedrichstr.

Kunstgewerbe Museum

str.

Film- mus.

Potsdamerpl.

Ⓢ

Leipziger

Leipzigerstr.

Charlotten

Kunstbibl.

Potsdamer

Platz

Platz

Museum für Kommunikation

Gemälde- galerie

Kupferstich- kabinett

Matthäi-

kirchpl.

Alte-

Ⓤ Potsdamerpl.

Daimler-Chrysler Contemporary

kstätte scher stand

Sigismundstr.

Stresemannstr.

Niederkirchnerstr. Zimmer-

Museum am Checkpoint Cha

Neue Nationalgalerie

Staatsbibliotek

Martin- Gropius-Bau

Kochstr.

Reichpietschufer

Köthenerstr.

Bernburgerstr.

Askanischerpl.

Anhalter-

Wilhelm-

Ⓤ Kochstr.

Schöneberger-

Sigismundstr.

str.

str.

str.

69

burger

z

Mendelssohn- Bartholdy-Park

Ⓤ

Mendelssohn- Bartholdy-Park

Ⓢ Anhalterbhf.

str.

Gemäldegalerie

OPEN	The gallery is open 10 am–6 pm, Tu–Wed, Fri–Sun; 10 am–10 pm, Thur.
CLOSED	Mon
CHARGES	Regular admission €6, reduced admission €3. Day ticket also covers the Neue Nationalgalerie (excluding special exhibitions), Hamburger Bahnhof, Kupferstichkabinett and Kunstgewerbe Museum. Free entry on Thur after 6 pm. No charge for children up to 16 years. Combined day ticket to all SMPK museums is €10 (reduced admission €5); three-day ticket to all SMPK museums €12 (reduced admission €6).
MAIN ENTRANCE	Kulturforum Potsdamerplatz, U or S to Mathäikirchplatz or Potsdamer Platz
TELEPHONE	266 2101
WEB	www.smb.spk-berlin.de
SERVICES	A buffet on the first floor serves cold and hot lunches, as well as tea, coffee and cakes, but it is overpriced.

HIGHLIGHTS

Cranach	Room 3
Holbein	Room 4
Breughel	Room 7
Rubens	Room 9
Rembrandt	Room 16/X
Vermeer	Room 18
Gainsborough	Room 20
Velázquez	Room XIII
Carravagio	Room XIV
Titian	Room XVI
Botticelli	Room XVIII
Raphael	Room 29

HISTORY OF THE COLLECTION

The Gemäldegalerie at the Kulturforum is Berlin's least publicised museum, but the collection of 13th–18th-C masterpieces is very impressive.

The gallery opened to the public in 1830, on the first floor of the newly built Schinkel Museum, above the antiquities collection. The collection was founded through purchases by the Prussian Royalty, in part supported by donations from wealthy citizens. A major part was purchased from the English merchant Edward Solly in 1821, including Raphael, Titian and Paris Bordone, and also Italian Quattrocento and Trecento painters, including Boticelli, Mantegna, Bellini and Giotto. The Solly collection also brought to Berlin early Dutch and German masters, including Holbein and van Eyck.

Further purchases concentrated on the Dutch and Flemish masters, above all Rembrandt and Rubens, and by the turn of the 20th C the collection had outgrown the Altes Museum. A new museum was built on the northern tip of the island, christened the Kaiser Friedrich Museum and renamed the Bode Museum.

After World War II, paintings rescued by the Allies from salt mines in Thuringia were shown first in Wiesbaden, then in Berlin Dahlem. Around 400 paintings were destroyed by an air-raid bunker fire; the remaining paintings in the eastern zone were rehoused in the Bode Museum.

In 1992 Berlin's municipal museums were unified, and in 1998 the collection moved to the Kulturforum. Modest from the exterior, the interior is a superb museum space, with the rooms in a semi-circle around the central hall. The exhibition is arranged topographically and chronologically, starting with early German painting on the right and Italian Trecento and Quattrocento painting on the left. With 850 paintings and 1,800 metres of hanging surface, you may wish to spread your visit over more than one day, by using the three-day pass.

13TH–16TH-C GERMAN PAINTING ROOMS I–III, 1–4

ROOM 1 begins with *Altar Tabel mit der Kreuzigung Christi* (1230/40), one of the oldest altarpieces in Germany. The left panel

GEMÄLDEGALERIE

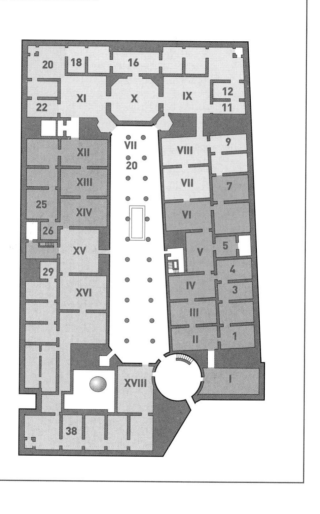

shows Christ brought before the high priest of Jerusalem (the city lies shrouded behind); the central panel has the crucified Christ surrounded by disciples, soldiers and onlookers; and the right panel an angel gesturing to Christ's empty tomb. *Thronende Madonna mit dem Kind* (1340/50) is regarded as the finest of its kind. Jesus was known in the Middle Ages as 'the new Solomon'; the unfinished wooden planks at the seat of the throne refer to the biblical description of Solomon's cedarwood throne.The kneeling figure is Ernst von Pardubitz, the first archbishop of Prague, who commissioned the painting.

ROOM 3 The German Renaissance master **Lucas Cranach the Elder** was a court painter who often took erotic subject matter from the classical literature widely read in the Humanist circles in which he moved. *Venus and Cupid as a Honey Thief* (1537) illustrates Theocritus' account of Cupid filching honey and getting stung by bees; when he ran to Venus for comfort, she compared his pain to the pangs of love. Notice Venus' contorted posture, a typical feature of the Mannerist style. *The Fountain of Youth* (1547) shows aged women in a rocky landscape entering a pool and emerging rejuvenated, amidst lush pastures. Notice Venus and Cupid as the fountain

Cranach the Elder *Lucrezia* (1533)

motif, and the couple in the bush, bottom right; details such as this would have appealed to his patrons.

ROOM 4 is outstanding for the portraits by **Hans Holbein the Younger**, including *Hermann Hillebrandt* (1533), *Duke Anton the Good of Lothringen* (c. 1543), and *Der Merchant Georg Gisze* (1532). The latter is especially well-known, and shows the Danzig-born cloth merchant Gisze, at the time employed in London at the trading post of the powerful Hanseatic League. Objects around his office and his rich clothing allude to his status, while the motto on the wall, 'there is no pleasure without a price', is apt for a trader in luxury goods. The flowers symbolise modesty and faithfulness in love, a token to his betrothed back in Germany, for whom the painting was commissioned.

14TH–16TH-C PAINTING FROM THE NETHERLANDS AND FRANCE ROOMS IV–VI, 5–7

ROOM IV has two outstanding altarpieces by **Rogier Van der Weyden**. *The Middleburger/Bladdelin Altar* (1445) was named after its donor Bladdelin, depicted in the left panel (he was chancellor of Burgundy and founder of the town of Middleburg). The central panel shows the birth of Christ; notice the pillar in the stable, which Mary leaned against while giving birth. Emperor Augustus is shown kneeling, repenting for having denied the divinity of Christ after being told by a seer about the miraculous birth. *Der Johannes Altar* (1453) depicts scenes from the life of John the Baptist. The left panel shows his birth and naming: his mother Elisabeth lies in bed, his father Zachariah records his name. The central panel shows John baptising Christ and the right panel shows Salome receiving John's head on a plate, while in the background, Salome's mother is stabbing it viciously. In *Christus im Haus des Pharisäers* by Dieric Bouts (c. 1640), Mary Magdalene has interrupted a dinner with Christ and some disciples. She weeps onto his feet, which she wipes with her hair and then anoints with oil. While the Pharisee and Peter are irritated by the intrusion, John is explaining the significance of the occasion to a cleric (the painting's donor). Bouts has created a powerful sense of depth, heightened by the figures gesturing towards the foreground and the objects on the table.

ROOM V *The Awakening of Lazarus* by **Aelbert van Outer** (c. 1450/60) is the only example of this artist's work. On the left, well-dressed Jews, who had come to offer their condolence, turn away in horror at the resurrected Lazarus, ignoring St. Peter's attempt to explain the significance of the miracle. The two paintings by **Hugo van der Goes** in this room are exceptional for their expressiveness and immediacy. *Die Anbetung der Hirten* (c. 1480) shows shepherds bursting in on the nativity, while Old Testament prophets open curtains to the scene. The sheaf of corn lying on the floor represents the sacrament. The texture and detail in *Der Anbetung der Könige* (1470) is remarkable: see for example the contrast between the smooth skin of the baby and the Magus' hands.

ROOM 5 has small but powerful portaits by **Jan van Eyck**, including *Baudouin de Lannoy* (c. 1436/38) and *Giovanni Arnolfini* (c. 1438). A different kind of expressivity is seen in *Bildnis einer jungen Dame* by Petrus Christus (1470), in which the sitter's features have an irregular beauty, enhanced by the artist's reduced formal range. Genre painting depicting everyday life became increasingly popular in the 17th C: in *Die Schach Partie* by **Lucas van Leyden** (c. 1508), the variation of chess being played is known as 'Courier', developed in Germany in the 13th C. From the man's expression, it seems that the woman has the upper hand; this follows the theme of feminine cunning the artist developed in previous series of engravings. *Parklandschaft mit Schloß* by **Hans Bol** (1589), painted in minute detail with gouache on parchment, belongs to a genre known as the 'cabinet miniature' The boy pumping up the ball is an allusion to the act of love and its consequences.

ROOM VI *Momus tadelt die Werke der Götter* by **Maerten van Heemskerk** (1561) illustrates an episode from Lucian, in which Momus, who personifies cynicism, upbraids the gods for their attempt to create the perfect work of art. Neptune has created a white horse, Vulcan a woman and Minerva a palace. The scroll attached to the base of the picture calls for a cavity to be built into the human chest in order to reveal the duplicitous heart; Momus holds a model taking this literally. Notice how he stands on stony ground, separated from the rest of the ensemble.

 Jean Bellagambe's horrifying *Triptych of the Last Judgement* (1520/25) shows the newly risen dead receiving their just deserts: Avarice, for example, is having molten gold poured down his throat. Notice the angel holding the mill stone, with dangling key, ready to seal hell for eternity. The saved are shown drinking from the well of life before ascending to the holy city of Jerusalem.

More worldly concerns feature in In *Marktfrau am Gemüsestand* (1567) by **Peter Aertsen**: the market stall holder spreads out her wares, while behind a couple fondle in a doorway. The painting's theme is the dangers of yielding to the senses, but the warning seems ambivalent.

ROOM 7 has *Die Niederlandische Sprichwörter* by **Peter Brueghel** (1551). Nicknamed 'Peter the Clown', Brueghell was the artistic heir of Hieronymus Bosch. Each of the hundred scenes from village life gone mad corresponds to a Dutch folk proverb; the upside-down globe on the left tells us nothing is as it should be. 'To drape the blue coat over your husband' is to deceive him; 'to throw roses to the pigs' is to be wasteful; 'to hang between heaven and earth' is to find yourself in a difficult position; 'to hold an eel by the tail' is to do something that's bound to fail; 'to carry the daylight out in a basket' is to waste time doing useless things; two people who 'crap from the same hole' are inseparable .

17TH-C FLEMISH AND DUTCH PAINTING
ROOMS VII–XI, 8–18
The following galleries contain some of the most famous paintings in the museum, and are primarily purchases from the Von Bode era.

ROOM 9 has *Bouquet of Flowers* by **Jan Brueghel the Elder** (1619/20), in which the artist painted the exotic flowers imported by his patrons Archdukes Albrecht and Isabella, and smaller works by **Peter Paul Rubens**, including *Das Kind mit dem Vögel* (1629/30). Rubens originally intended that the child (recently identified as his nephew) be seen as an angel—the bird was an afterthought.

ROOM VIII has larger works by Rubens. In *St. Cecilia* (1639/40), the patron saint of music looks up towards the source of divine harmony. The violet, green and orange that compose the secondary triad enhance one another; Rubens took an interest in colour theory, which related colour combinations to musical chords.

ROOM VII has some vivid still lives. *Still Life with Lobster and Fruit* by **Frans Snyders** represents earthly desires with the lobster, capercaillie and plucked chicken, while Christ and paradise are denoted by grapes and strawberries.

Portrait of a Genoese Lady, by **Anthony van Dyck** (1619/20), though apparently a companion piece to *Portrait of a Genoese Gentleman*, was painted twenty years later; the handling of paint, particularly in the lace work at the collar, is more delicate, and she sits further back within the frame.

Moving through **ROOMS XI, 11 AND 12**, past genre painting and Dutch landscapes—typified by *Holländische Flachlandschaft* by **Philips Koninck** 1655/60—we arrive at **ROOM 13**, with Frans Hals, the most influential Dutch painter before Rembrandt. His painterly, spontaneous style is typified in *Malle Babbe* (1633/35). The owl sitting on the crone's shoulder stands for wisdom, but also, as a creature of the night, for dark forces; the pewter tankard speaks for itself.

ROOM 16 brings us to the museum's **Rembrandt** collection.

In *Joseph and Potiphar's Wife* (1655) it is the marriage bed, scene of the crime, that is lit; the king, confronting his wife, and Joseph, gesturing despairingly, recede into the shadows.

Continuing into **ROOM X**, we find *Self Portrait with Velvet Beret and Fur-Collared Coat* (1634). Rembrandt painted self-portraits throughout his career; in this one, made shortly after his marriage, he wears the trademark beret and adopts the inquisitive, half-turned pose typical of Renaissance paintings of artists. In *Moses with the Ten Commandments* (1659), Moses, brought dramatically up against the pictorial frame, is about to smash the stone tablets in distress. The colour range is reduced almost entirely to monochrome and detail is neglected in favour of painterly marks.

ROOM 18 **Vermeer**'s reputation is based on only 35 paintings, three of which can be seen here. In Vermeer's *Young Woman with Pearl Necklace* (1662/65), the viewer's gaze meets the blank back wall, creating perpendicular tension with the woman's gaze. The upward trajectory of our gaze and the cut-off chair also create depth and an illusion of sharing the space. *The Glass of Wine* (1661/62) shows a dashing young man offering a seated woman a second glass of wine: she is shyly avoiding his gaze, but her apparent breathlessness and parted legs suggest arousal. The stringed instrument on the chair, a chitarrone, represents frivolity, though the painting can also be understood as an appeal for moderation. Vermeer made use of the 'camera obscura', which projected a scene onto a canvas, enabling artists to reach greater heights of verisimilitude but also a slightly fish-eyed effect.

18TH-C FRENCH, ENGLISH AND GERMAN PAINTING
ROOMS 20–22

ROOM 20 has **Gainsborough**'s *The Marsham Children* (1787), commissioned by Charles Marsham, the 1st Earl of Romney. His son Charles stands apart from his sisters, reflecting his status as heir. Landscape is depicted as place for play, and a timeless atmosphere pervades. Painted in relaxed brushstrokes, the painting is nevertheless tightly composed. The faces would have been added after separate portrait sittings, which explains why the children's gazes fail to meet convincingly.

Joshua Reynolds' *George Clive and his Family with Indian Servant* (c. 1765/66) is a painting divided between inside and outside, each setting representing the roles of the sexes. After making a fortune in East India, Clive had returned to England and married Sidney Bolton. Their child, born in 1764, died young. She was to have formed the painting's centrepiece; instead, the father was added and the painting became an epitaph. Reynold's handling of the expensive Indian silk of the women's garments is luscious, though the hard lines elsewhere add a more formal tone.

ROOM 21 In **Jean Antoine Watteau**'s identically sized paintings, *Die Französische Komödie* and *Die Italienische Komödie* (1716), the two national dramatic forms are compared. French comedy relied on set pieces with musical interludes, while Italian comedy, or commedia dell'arte, relied on stock characters and improvisation. Both paintings feature well-known actors of the time. Among the French spectators are Bacchus, wearing a leopardskin, and Cupid.

ROOM 22 contains Friedericiana, art produced in and around the court of Friederich the Great. The Prussian court painter **Antoine Pesne**'s *Friedrich the Great as Crown Prince* (1739/40) established the standard form for representing a ruler.

In *Self Portrait with Henriette Joyard and Marie de Rège at the Easel* (1754), Pesne and his two daughters form an intimate family triangle. Warm colours are set against pastel shades, a technique that influenced on Rococo painting during the period. In *Selbstbildnis* (1776/77), **Anna Dorothea Therbusch**, a Berlin painter, depicts herself as a Vestal Virgin, whose austere existence reflected Therbusch's own existence as a woman painter.

Now is a good point to take a break. Once you're ready to start again, go to Room XVIII, on your left as you look down the central hall.

13TH–16TH-C ITALIAN PAINTING
ROOMS XV–XVIII, 29–41

Working through the 13th–16th-C Italian collections chronologically means you must walk through the rooms in reverse numerical order. We begin in the Quattrocento with **ROOM XVIII**. *Venus, Mars and Cupid* (1505) lie amidst nature: a rabbit nuzzles up to Venus while doves play a love game in the foreground. The paraphernalia of war, scattered about the landscape, are being carried away by amoretti: Neo-Platonism valued the union between Venus and Mars as a union of opposites and symbol of fertility. Nearby are a number of works by **Botticelli**, including *Maria with Child, Singing* (1477).

The room has two paintings interesting for their use of perspective, a burgeoning science during the early Renaissance. In an *Annunciation* by **Piero del Pollaiuolo** (c.1470), the figures appear to float in front of the decorative background, while the field opens up to a view of Florence and the Tuscan hills. **Francesco di Giorgio Martini**'s *Architectural Veduta* (1490/1500), a more accurate perspective, was designed to be set into a wall panel. Walking back and forth in front of the painting creates interesting effects—don't worry, the docents are used to it!

ROOM 38 has **Andrea Mantegna**'s *Mary with the Sleeping Child*, in which Mantegna uses line to bind together the forms of Mary and the child. At the other extreme is *Madonna with Saints* (1488/89) by **Carlo Crivelli**, with its overlapping, patterned fields. Crivelli had a highly individual painterly language: note the archaic almond eyes, flattened noses and veined foreheads, along with the trompe l'oeil fruit, including the ubiquitous cucumber.

Through the hallway (Room 35), we reach the miniatures in Room 34 and the digital gallery in Room 33, which provides background information on selected paintings.

ROOM 29 brings you to the Madonna paintings by **Raphael**. The latest of the paintings, *Madonna Colonna* (c. 1508), shows clear departures from earlier versions: the palette is lighter and the forms are more delicately modelled, the horizon has become lower and Mary's hair has turned from brown to blonde.

IN ROOM XVI is **Titian**'s *Venus with the Organ Player* (1550/52), one of the last great 16th-C paintings to have been purchased by Wilhelm von Bode in Vienna. In it, a well-dressed cavalier plays the organ to the naked Venus. *Mary with the Child Venerated by Two Evangelists* (1570/75) was painted by **Tintoretto** and shows Mary as Woman of the Apocalypse, appearing to the Evangelists in a vision.

ROOM XV holds **Correggio**'s *Leda and the Swan* (1532), one of a series of four depicting the exploits of Zeus. In 1721 it was acquired by Philipe d'Orléan, whose son Louis found it offensive and tore it up, destroying Leda's head. Reassembled by the court painter, it was purchased in 1765 by Friedrich the Great for Sanssouci, where Leda's head was repainted by Jacob Schlesinger.

17TH- AND 18TH-C ITALIAN, GERMAN, FRENCH AND SPANISH PAINTNG ROOMS XII–XIV, 24–26

ROOM XIV has a number of paintings by **Caravaggio**, including *Cupid as Victor* (1601/2). The symbols of art, science and power lie at Cupid's feet, his grin seemingly mocking the peaks of human attainment. The painting's homoeroticism guaranteed its notoriery; notice too Cupid's dirty toenails, a lifelike detail (Caravaggio used street children as models).

ROOM XIII *Portrait of a Lady* (1630/33) by **Diego Velázquez** is thought to show Countess Monterrey, wife of the Spanish ambassador in Rome. Velázquez abandoned the stark lighting contrasts of the earlier *Three Musicians* (1616/20) in favour of subtle half-tones: the sitter, blurred on close inspection, seems to be seen across a dust-filled room.

The highlights of **ROOM XII** are the four veduti, or view paintings, by **Canaletto**, commissioned in 1763 by Sigismund Streit, a Berlin merchant based in Venice.

ROOM 24 **Sebastiano Ricci**'s *Bathsheba Bathing* (1725) sheds the moralising aspects attached to the story until the 16th C, so that only the eroticism of the scene remains. It was originally thought to show Venus bathing: only the messenger on the left, bringing David's summons, enabled the subject to be identified. Friedrich the Great purchased the painting believing it was a Veronese, so indebted is Ricci's colouration to the master.

ROOM 25 contains French landscape painting by **Nicolas Poussin** and **Claude Lorrain**. Poussin's *Landscape with the Evangelist Matthew* (1639/40) achieves its solid feel through the architectural fragments and warm, muted colour. Lorrain, in contrast, was a painter of light, with a fundamentally decorative style, seen in *Italian Coast* (1642).

ROOM 26 has the exceptional *Farmers Eating Peas* by **Georges de la Tour** (1622/25). Influenced by Caravaggio's half-length figures, La Tour painted the poor around his home of Lorraine. Popular during his lifetime, the artist was forgotten and only rediscovered in the early 19th C.

Neue Nationalgalerie

OPEN	The gallery is open 10 am–6 pm, Tue, Weds and Fri; 10 am–10 pm, Thur; 11 am–6 pm, Sat–Sun.
CLOSED	Mon
CHARGES	€6/€3 day ticket covers all Tiergarten museums, with audio guide. Combined day ticket to all SMPK museums is €10 (reduced admission €5); three-day ticket to all SMPK museums €12 (reduced admission €6).
MAIN ENTRANCE	Potsdamer Straße 50
TELEPHONE	266 2662
WEB	www.smb.spk-berlin.de
SERVICES	Cloakroom
SHOP	The museum shop on the lower level is small, but has a good collection of catalogues, monographs and art books.

HIGHLIGHTS

Edvard Munch's *Melancholy*

E.L. Kirchner's *Potsdamer Platz*

Otto Dix's *Card Players*

George Grosz's *Pillar of Society*

Wolfgang Matthauer's *A Wide Field*

Gerhard Richter's *Curtain III (Light)*

Sigmar Polke East's *Community Project Improvement*

Adolph Menzel

Art at the Turn of the Century

The Neue Nationalgalerie houses 20th-C modern art (the Alte Nationalgalerie has 19th-C and the Hamburger Bahnhof contemporary art). The collection was established during the Cold War as a replacement for the Nationalgalerie in East Berlin.

Happily, after German reunification, the two partially overlapping collections were combined.

The history of some individual works in the collection is spectacular: many paintings were purged by the Nazis as 'degenerate' only to be reacquired in the 1970s and 1980s. Other pieces that were 'lost' during the war resurfaced in West Germany and slowly percolated back into the collection.

The building, designed by Mies van der Rohe in 1968, looks like a factory polished to a high sheen and put on a pedestal. In fact, Mies's last major building is as much a work of art in itself as a building for display.

THE COLLECTION

The strength of the museum's permanent collection lies in the visual dialogue created between artists working over the same time period in West Germany, East Germany and the United States.

The Neue Nationalgalerie

The earliest works mark the beginnings of what would come to be known as Expressionism. Artists such as **Edvard Munch**, in his painting *Melancholy* (1906–07), began to distance themselves from the decorative, organic style of Art Nouveau painters. In *Melancholy*, large swathes of exposed canvas and sparse brushwork seem to lend to the motif a lonely emptiness. (The painting was removed from the collection of the Nationalgalerie by Herman Göring in 1937 and sold; it could only be reacquired in 1997.)

Paired portraits by **Oskar Kokoschka** of *Adolf Loos* (1909) and *Bessie Loos* (1910) can be read as an open declaration of rebellion against the controlled structures and ornamental styles of fin-de-siecle Vienna. Kokoschka's expressionistic style of painting was considered scandalous because of the violence of his brushstrokes, his unconventional forms and the 'irrationality' of his compositions. In these portraits, the studied, balled energy of Loos is complemented by the thinness and transparency of Bessie, his second wife, who was consumptive. Loos, a modern architect who advocated clean lines and functional designs, was Kokoschka's only supporter during this early phase of his career. Legend has it that the artist often earned money by wagering on his ability to drink visitors under the table.

One characteristic of German Expressionist painting is the application of brash, bold colour and brushstroke to the subject-matter of traditional painting. **Emile Nolde**'s interpretation of *Pfingsten* (1909), which depicts the scene from Pentecost where the apostles are visited by the Holy Spirit, is a good example. In a later interview, Nolde said, his 'aim was to show in strong visual form that a community of passionate men can be ready at any moment to go to their deaths for the truth'.

Another traditional genre is the self-portrait. *Self Portrait with Monocle* (1910) by **Karl Schmidt-Rottluff** is a painting of the artist as performer. Schmidt-Rottluff obscures his gaze with a monocle and places himself on a stage, marking the ambivalent relationship between painter and audience.

E. L. Kirchner *Potsdamer Platz* (1914)

Rottluff was part of the Dresden art circle called *die Brücke* ('the Bridge'), along with other painters exhibited in the Neue Nationalgalerie, such as Nolde and **Ernst Ludwig Kirchner** (see picture on p. 85). The subjects of Kirchner's work are the grandiose buildings, dance halls and prostitutes that were to be found on the Potsdamer Platz of Weimar Berlin. The world in his art hardly resembles the cleaned-up, corporate space that surrounds the Neue Nationalgalerie today.

The collection also includes some early works by Dada artist **Hannah Höch** and **Kurt Schwitters**. Höch's *Cut with a Kitchen Knife* (1919-20) is a photomontage and collage that pokes fun at Weimar politicians, scientists and businessmen. It was considered the best work at the First International Dada Exhibition of 1920.

Schwitters' *The Wide Schmurchel* (1923) is a 'found object' piece, collected from driftwood and remnants of oars the artist found on the beach while on vacation with fellow Dadaists Höch and Jean Arp. It is one of the few remaining works in what Schwitters called his 'relief-assemblage' style.

Several of the works in the collection are concerned with war and its consequences. *The Fallen* (1915–1916), a sculpture in bronze by **Wilhelm Lehmbruck**, depicts a naked soldier with elongated limbs, 'stretched' in an arch over the ground, as if his body had become a bridge between life and death. The critique of war and militarism became even more pronounced in the interwar years. **Otto Dix**'s *Card Players* (1920) is a condemnation of the horrors of World War I and of the blind militarism and chauvinism that persisted in Weimar Germany. The mutated, prosthetic veterans he depicts seem to carry on mindlessly with the same ideas that are responsible for their own sorry state.

Georg Grosz turned his attention to the hypocrisy and idiocy of the ruling classes in *Pillar of Society* (1926), a visual pun on Heinrich Ibsen's play of the same name. His sense of caricature reaches its pinnacle in this piece—he depicts a newspaper editor with a chamber pot on his head to show the narrow-mindedness of his ideas, a lawyer with a swastika on his lapel and visions of the Crusaders in his head, and a drunken military chaplain. In the background, ruthless skeleton soldiers march towards their destruction. Dix and Grosz both served in World War I, and Dix was arrested and put in jail in for two weeks as a suspect in a plot to assassinate Hitler. Grosz latter immigrated to the United States.

The gallery's collection of post-World War II art is a compilation of works originally collected in the GDR and works that were collected in the FRG during the Cold War. The inclusion of East German artist **Werner Trübke** in the collection was a controversial move, since some of his paintings are considered by many to be socialist propaganda. The painting *Dr Schulze's Memories of Life* (1965), however, is the third attempt in a series of eleven to understand the psyche of a Nazi executioner. Trübke uses imagery reminiscent of Hieronymus Bosch to depict his subject's fantastic and gruesome imagination.

Wolfgang Mattheuer was one of the few GDR artists respected both in the East and in the West. His landscapes, including *A Wide Field* (1973), work dark, ominous shadows into corners and along horizons of the picture plane, creating bucolic scenes that are fragile and filled with a sense of unease.

Curtain III (Light) (1965), by **Gerhard Richter**, plays with the relationship between photography and painting, creating a painted image that seems to make the material object dissolve into light, thereby achieving in paint a promise held out by photography.

Sigmar Polke's *Community Project Improvement East* (1991) is one of the few pieces in the collection concerned with the contradictions and ironies of German reunification. Consisting of a thin membrane stretched across wooden supports and depicting a large diagonal arrow pointing upwards, it calls into question the stability of the 'project of improving East Germany economically. The technique Polke uses is reminiscent of a style he developed in the 1960s called Capitalist Realism, an ironic take on American Pop art that is deliberately sloppy, revealing the methods by which slick capitalist images are produced. Here, he uses a thick black pen to 'mark' the project of economic recovery.

Hamburger Bahnhof Museum for the Contemporary

OPEN   The museum is open 10 am–6 pm, Tue–Fri; 11 am–10 pm, Sat; 11 am– 6 pm, Sun.

CLOSED   Mon

CHARGES   Regular admission €6, reduced €3 (includes audio guide). Free entry on Thursdays after 2 pm (no audio guide). Day ticket also covers the Neue Nationalgalerie (excluding special exhibitions), Gemaldegalerie, Kupferstichkabinett and Kunstgewerbe Museum. No charge for children up to 16 years. Combined day ticket to all SMPK museums is €10 (reduced admission €5); three-day ticket to all SMPK museums €12 (reduced admission €6).

TEL   39 78 34 12

WEB   www.smb.spk-berlin.de

ADDRESS   Invaliden Straße 50/51

U-BAHN   U 6 Zinnowitzer Straße

S-BAHN   S3/5/7/9 Lehrter Stadtbahnhof

SHOP   There is a large and well-stocked bookshop for contemporary art and theory.

EATING   The Restaurant Sarah Wiener (€€, 70 71 36 50) is the perfect place to recharge. It is spacious, with both tables and a lounge area for reading the papers, as well as a patio facing into the courtyard on one side and the area over canal on the other. The menu changes daily and is described as 'German International': a meal with drinks will cost in the region of €15 a head. On Sunday mornings the restaurant fills for brunch.

HIGHLIGHTS

Joseph Beuys   West Wing
Anselm Kiefer   Main Hall
Cy Twombly
Robert Rauschenberg
Andy Warhol

THE BUILDING

The Hamburger Bahnhof Museum for the Contemporary, with art from the 1960s to the present, is the third of the trio of national art galleries in Berlin. The building, tucked away at the northern edge of Tiergarten, is the former end station of the Hamburg-Berlin railway. It was built in 1846–47 in a late Classical style. After the war, the building was operated and staffed by the East German railway. Handed over to the West Berlin Senate in 1983, it was restored in 1987 by Winnetou Kampmann.

The building meets the demand for space created by the purchase of new collections of contemporary art, in particular that of Erich Marx. In 1994, Paul Kleihaus designed two new wings; only the east wing has been completed. The building opened in its current incarnation in 1996.

THE WEST WING
JOSEPH BEUYS

The works of **Joseph Beuys** in the West Wing can be seen as expressions of his *Gesamtkunstwerk*. To the first-time viewer they seem arcane and unsettling; familiarity with the theoretical background helps, but the strangeness is irreducible and the meaning of Beuys' art remains beyond our ability to articulate.

The End of the 20th Century (1982–83) is a smaller version of the monumental sculpture *7000 Oaks*, created for the Kassel Documenta VIII. Beuys understood the *End of the 20th Century* as the end of the age of materialism. The basalt blocks accompany the trees as a symbol of the inorganic: the trolley and chisel are left to emphasise the fact that the rocks have been removed from the earth. The work seems connected to Beuys' affinity to the Green movement, which became a force in mainstream German politics during the 1980s.

Beuys' theory of art revolved around 'social plasticity', the idea that the individual treats his or her own life, and hence surroundings, as art. *Unschlitt* (1977), in the main room of the West Wing, is blocks of wax that take their form from a pedestrian walkway, a piece of architecture that for Beuys embodied urban

HAMBURGER BAHNHOF

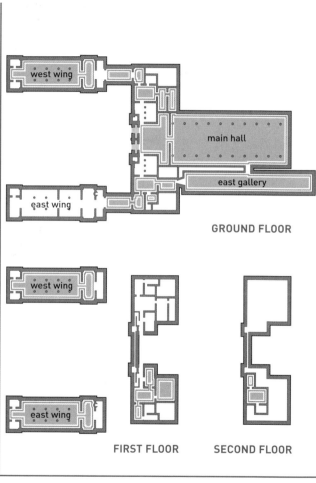

west wing

main hall

east gallery

east wing

GROUND FLOOR

west wing

east wing

FIRST FLOOR   **SECOND FLOOR**

depersonalisation. The moulding process, requiring twenty tonnes of molten wax, was a complicated undertaking, since the wax cooled on the outside faster than on the inside. For Beuys the heat represented an animation of the 'frozen' social structure. The sculpture only cooled fully weeks after the exhibition had ended.

Tram Stop (1979) is an associative assemblage that refers to a monument at a tram stop in Beuys' home town commemorating the battle of Nassau. The combination brings to mind human suffering, war, and the course of history.

Beuys' drawings and diagrams, by-products of what he called his 'permanent dialogue' with the public, are hung on the walls. The board produced in 1973 was created during his collaboration with the Glaswegian gangster-turned-sculptor Jimmy Boyle.

THE MAIN HALL
ANSELM KIEFER

Anselm Kieifer studied under Beuys at the Düsseldorf Academy of Art and his work shares Beuys' materiality as well as his fascination and dread of the irrational. However, Kiefer was less concerned with the unconscious than with history; his narrative concerns make him a more traditional painter and sculptor.

Weg der Weltweisheit: die Hermann Schlacht (1980) refers to the defeat of Napoleon's troops at the Teutoberg forest in 1816. Kiefer has populated the dense forest with artists and intellectuals, who hailed the victory as a demonstration of German national strength. But the fire threatens to burn out of control, making the work both a homage and a cautionary tale.

In 1989 Kiefer refused to take part in a state census. *Volkszählung* (1991), with its working title '60 million peas', is a statement about a state apparatus that reduces its citizens to pea-like counters. Folk memory, and especially the cultural memory of Jewish intellectuals murdered or driven from Germany, is represented by the archive of lead books.

The title of *Mohn und Gedächtnis* (Poppies and Memory) (1989) is taken from the book of poetry by Paul Celan. The poppies stand for intoxication and dreams, sprouting from between the pages of lead books. These press down on the wings of the aircraft, symbolising the flight of fancy. Lead is the material historically associated with Saturn, the planetary symbol of war, death and defeat; Kiefer's art has aptly been characterised as 'saturnine'. The paintings around the main hall feature Kiefer's use of straw, ashes and earth, often with charred surfaces, recalling the scorched-earth strategy of the German troops during their retreat from Russia in 1943.

MARIO MERZ

Mario Merz was a leading figure in the 'Arte Povera' movement, which reverted to simple means and materials in a reaction to the rapid industrialisation of Northern Italy during the 1970s and 1980s. He described art after 1966 as 'a long Sunday', during which artists did no real work, but merely dismantle the achievements of previous decades. Merz developed an idiosyncratic vocabulary, in which the recurring igloo form is interpreted as a metaphor for the human mind. *La Goccia d'Acqua* (1987) is a glass dome supporting numbers made from neon tubing. These form the Fibonacci series, in which each number is the sum of the two preceding it (the series is common in nature and was derived from observations of rabbits breeding). An extended table runs through the igloo, at the narrow end of which is a tap dripping water.

DONALD JUDD

Donald Judd was the leading exponent of the 'what you see is what you get' school of North American Minimalism, a gesture of liberation from the perceived constraints of European representational art. Judd's sculpture was made from industrial materials, finished to commercial production standards. Criticisms that he glossed over social conflict and reproduced wholesale the capitalist aesthetic are probably unwarranted; Judd was a utopianist who produced mutedly elegant objects with a high degree of sculptural form. Notice the contrast of surfaces and materials that draw attention to physical presence.

CY TWOMBLY

Like Beuys, **Cy Twombly** is concerned with prehistory and the limits of the verbal. When compared with the bravado of the

Abstract Expressionists or the utilitarianism of the Minimalists, one can see why Twombly has been called the most 'un-American of American painters'. During the 1950s he worked as a cryptographer for the US military, though he admitted he was too vague to be much good at it. Like many of his contemporaries, Twombly also had an interest in Mexican and Native American art. *Free Wheeler* (1955) features pencil scribbles resembling archaic calligraphy.

Thyrsis (1977) refers to Theocrites' idyllic poem in which Thyrsis sang to a goatherd about Daphnis' love. The painting's triptych form also alludes to religious paintings of the Middle Ages.

ROBERT RAUSCHENBERG

Robert Rauschenberg, like Twombly, was from the American south. They were contemporaries at the Black Mountain College, a hotbed of experimentalism in the early 1950s that influenced composer John Cage and poet Charles Olson.

Rauschenberg became one of Pop Art's forerunners. *Homage to David Tudor* (1961) was created during a performance at the US embassy in Paris. During the production, David Tudor played a piece by John Cage on the cello; a machine created by Jean Tinguely jumped across a stage discarding metal parts; a painting by Niki de Saint Phalle was shot. A microphone relayed this to Rauschenberg, painting in his hotel room. When an alarm clock went off, a porter emerged from Rauschenberg's hotel carrying the finished painting. *Stripper* (1962) refers to Tinguely's machine.

The Frightened Gods of Fortune (1981) dates from the period overshadowed by the arms race, and reflects Rauschenberg's involvement in civil rights, peace and environmental movements. The images on the ladder start with George Washington, first US president, at the top, and lead to a skeleton at the base. Poisonous snakes and insects suggest mutation and nuclear landscapes. *Red China Green House* (1984) emerged from the Rauschenberg Overseas Cultural Exchange (ROCI), Rauschenberg's collaboration with artists around the world.

ANDY WARHOL

Andy Warhol undermined the myth of the uniqueness of the work of art, not to mention the artist, and turned the pioneering, existentialist ethos of the preceding generation of painters on its head. *Ambulance Disaster* (1963) locates the image's loss of power to shock in its mass reproduction. Questions about self and authenticity are addressed in *Double Elvis* (1963), which also ventures into the darker regions of celebrity infatuation. Later works, such as the huge *Mao* (1973), plays with the assimilation of icons in pop-cultural iconography; the imperfect appearance of his work can be interpreted as irony.

FIRST FLOOR

The first floor of the west wing shows works from the **Erich Marx** collection, shown in rotation, and works by **Gerhard Richter**, **Sigmar Polke**, **Georg Baselitz**, **A.R.Penck**, **Thomas Struth** and **Thomas Ruff**, alongside international artists including **Rachel Whiteread**, **Damian Hirst**, **Bruce Naumann**, **Julian Schnabel**, **Robert Wilson**, **Bill Viola**, **Jeff Koons**, **Cindy Shermann** and **Rebecca Horn**. The first floor of the east wing is given over to temporary exhibitions of contemporary art.

in the area

POTSDAMER PLATZ AND KULTURFORUM
U OR S TO POTSDAMER PLATZ

Daimler Chrysler Contemporary Alte Potsdamer Straße 5, Haus Huth, 25 941 420, www.collection.daimlerchrysler.com. Open 11 am–6 pm, guided tours 3 pm Sat. Collection specialises in abstract/geometric/minimalist painting, now with 600 m3 of exhibition space. **Map p. 69, 2C**

Filmmuseum Berlin Potsdamer Straße 2, 300 90 30, www.filmmuseum-berlin.de. 10 am–6 pm, Tue–Su, 10 am–10 pm, Thur. German film history, from pioneer cinema and silent film to Weimar Republic and exile in Hollywood; also postwar and contemporary. With a special focus on Marlene Dietrich. **Map p. 69, 2C**

The Holocaust Memorial

Gedenkstätte Deutscher Widerstand Stauffenbergstraße 13–14, 26 99 50 00, www.gdw-berlin.de. 9 am–6 pm, Mon–Wed; 9 am–6 pm, Fri; 10 am–6 pm, Sat–Sun. Free entry. The former military headquarters of the Third Reich, documenting resistance to the Nazi regime, culminating in Stauffenberg's assassination attempt on Hitler in 1944. Unfortunately in German only, though with ample photographic material. The rooms themselves are interesting, with the original flooring with swastika bordering. **Map p. 69, 1C**

Holocaust Memorial Wilhlemstraße/Ebertstraße, 26 39 43 11, www.holocaust-mahnmal.de. This controversial monument to Jewish victims of the Holocaust was designed by Peter Eisenmann. Progress was halted in 2005 when the manufacturers of the graffiti remover used to clean the slabs were found to have been linked to the production of Zyklon B. Then Eisenmann, who himself lost family members in the Holocaust, got into trouble for a remark and had to apologise. Additionally, the stone slabs, arranged at different heights, have failed to achieve the hoped-for wave effect. **Map p. 69, B2**

Kupferstichkabinett (Collection of Drawings and Graphics)
Matthäikirchplatz 8, 266 20 02, www.smb.spk-berlin.de. 10 am–6 pm, Tue–Fri; 11 am–6 pm, Sat–Sun. A comprehensive collection of graphic

art, with works ranging from Botticelli to Joseph Beuys. Sections on illustrated books and manuscripts, drawings and prints. Also mounts temporary exhibitions. **Map p. 69, 1C**

Kunstbibliotek Matthäikirchplatz 6, 266 20 29, www.smb.spk-berlin.de. 10 am–6 pm, Tue–Fri; 11 am– 6 pm, Sat–Sun. Reading room open 9 am–10 pm, Mon–Fri; study room open 2 pm–10 pm, Mon, and 9 am–4 pm, Tue–Fri. **Map p. 69, 1C**

Kunstgewerbe Museum Tiergartenstraße 6, 266 29 02, www.smb.spk-berlin.de. 10 am–6 pm, Tue–Fri; 11 am– 6 pm, Sat–Sun. Applied arts and crafts from the Middle Ages to the present day. The lower gound floor has a collection of industrial products of particular significance to contemporary design practice. **Map p. 69, 1C**

Musikinstrumenten-Museum Tiergartenstraße 1, 25 48 11 39, www.sim.spk-berlin.de. 9 am–5 pm, Tue–Fri; 9 am–10 pm, Thur; 10 am–5 pm, Sat–Sun. European musical instruments from the 16th to the 20th C (attached to the Berlin Philarmonie). With over 3,000 more in storage, it's one of the most comprehensive in the world. **Map p. 69, 2C**

Staatsbibliotek Potsdamer Straße 33, 030 26 60, www.stabikat.de. 9 am–9 pm, Mon–Fri; 9 am–5 pm, Sat. Hans Sharoun's last big building, finished in 1978, took eleven years to construct. The spectacular interior, with its coloured glass tiles and open-floor plan, featured in a scene from Wim Wenders' film *Wings of Desire*. Entry to main hall is free, weekly reading tickets cost €2.50 (ID needed). **Map p. 69, 2C**

Public art at Potsdamer Platz

There are several public sculptures belonging to Daimler Chrysler, which has its headquarters here, including *Riding Bikes* by **Robert Rauschenberg** in the courtyard of Haus Huth. The artist has upended two ubiquitous Berlin bicycles and lit them in neon, a celebration of the bike as eco-friendly means of transport par excellence. On Marlene-Dietrich-Platz, in front of the Casino, is *Balloon Flower* (2000) by **Jeff Koons**, in which the king of kitsch puns on gravity with this four-and-a-half-ton steel balloon shape. Around the corner on Eichhornstraße is *Boxers* (1987) by **Keith Haring**. Installed in 1998, the 5-m blue and red cut-out figures by the legendary US graffiti artist provide a pop flavour to the Kulturforum. If you walk in the other direction and look up at the roof of the Debis building on

Schelling Straße, you'll see what looks like a home-made space craft come to grief. It's in fact a work entitled *Landed* by **Auke de Vries** (2002). A trumpet sticks out of the cockpit at an awkward angle and a banner flies from the back, as if the craft has become detached from some intergalactic parade. The artist has said he aims to react to scientific developments, relativity theory and bio-politics. How *Landed* achieves this is unsure, but it's probably the most unusual and humorous piece of public art in Berlin.

PARISER PLATZ AND REGIERUNGS VIERTEL
S TO UNTER DEN LINDEN

Akademie der Künste Pariser Platz 4, Tel 39 07 61 55, www.adk.de. 11 am–6 pm, Tue–Wed, Fri, Sun; 11 am–8 pm, Sun. This venue for high-brow, left-of-centre art and performance has, after interminable delays, moved into new, ultra-modern quarters at its prewar location on Pariser Platz. Free entry 1st Sun of the month. **Map p. 69, 2B**

Brandenburger Tor Pariser Platz. Built in 1791 to a design by Carl Langhans, it has seen a great deal of historical turbulence. It was badly damaged in the war, was inside the Russian zone and the Berlin wall ran just in front of it. The Prussian cross was removed by the Communists and returned after reunification. At New Year the Tor is the scene of extravagant partying. **Map p. 69, 2B**

Kanzleramt (Federal Chancellery) Willy-Brandt-Straße. Designed by Berlin architects Axel Schultes and Charlotte Frank and completed in 2001, the Chancellery is a breathtaking construction based around a central building and two long office wings. A radical departure from the Prussian building tradition, it suggests movement and transparency, and from ground level is oddly difficult to grasp as a whole. A walk around the entire building is worthwhile: there is a pleasant walkway ending at the beer garden behind the Haus der Kulturen. **Map p. 69, 1B**

Lehrter Stadtbahnhof Viewing Point on Invalidenstraße. Berlin's last big building project: when finished, the former central station will once again be Berlin's major rail terminus. The five levels will provide 70,000 m2 of commercial space, drastically redefining the infrastructural void between the east and the west. **Map p. 69, 1A**

Marie-Elisabeth Lüders Building (Bundestag) Designed by Munich architect Stephen Braunfels, Schiffbauerdamm stands exactly where the

The Reichstag dome from the inside

wall ran, and original sections of the wall have been integrated into the ground floor rooms. **Map p. 69, 2B**

Paul Löbe Building (Bundestag) Paul Löbe Allee. This building, also by Braunfels, sits opposite the Kanzleramt. It's recognisable by the glass façade and 23-m projecting roof. **Map p. 69, B2**

The Reichstag Platz der Republik. 8 am–10 pm every day. Norman Foster's dome, built between 1995 and 1999, is Berlin's most visited attraction: unless you come promptly at opening time the queue stretches around the block. It's an interesting experience in democratic architecture—views down into the body of the building allow you to watch the Bundestag in session. A photographic history of the building charts its fortunes, inextricably bound up with German nation since its construction in 1894. Roof restaurant (226 29 20). **Map p. 69, B2**

GOING WEST

Bauhaus-Archiv Museum für Gestaltung Klingelhöferstraße 14, 254 00 20, www.bauhaus.de. 10 am–5 pm, Wed–Mon. A late construction by Bauhaus founder Walter Gropius, built between 1976 and 1979. The permanent exhibition shows works of architecture, furniture, graphics, ceramics, metalwork, photography and stage design. The Bauhaus shop sells a selection of 250 modern reproductions of original objects. *U* to Nollendorfplatz; bus 100, 129 187 or 341 to Lützowplatz **Map p. 68, 3C**

Haus der Kulturen der Welt John Foster Dulles Allee 10, 397 87 0, www.hkw.de. 9 am–1 am every day. Built in 1957 by US architect Hugh Stubbins, the House of World Cultures is affectionately termed 'the pregnant oyster' by Berliners for its convex white roof. It's a venue for world music, lectures, and art installations by class international acts. The Auster Café at the back of the building offers secluded Spree views. *S* to Unter den Linden, bus 100 **Map p. 69, 2B**

Haus der Kulturen

Kunstforum der Berliner Volksbank Budapester Straße 35, 30 63 17 17, www.berliner-volksbank.de. 10 am–6 pm, Tue–Sun. Temporary exhibitions showcasing collections from other museums. *U* to Wittenbergplatz **Map p. 68, 2C**

Siegessäule am Großer Stern Straße 17 Juni, 391 29 61. Open 1.30 pm–6.30 pm,

Apr–Oct; 9.30 am–6.30 pm, Nov–Mar. It's an incredible thought, but the immense Victory Column was actually moved by Hitler from in front of the Reichstag to its present position at the crossroads in the centre of the Tiergarten. Climb to the top and in summer see the Tiergarten enveloped in cloud of barbeque smoke. A walk around the Tiergarten is highly recommended too: with its winding paths and surprising vistas, it is an oasis of calm. *U* to Unter den Linden, bus 100 **Map p. 68, 3B**

commercial galleries

Galerie Georg Nothelfer im Tiergartendreieck Corneliusstraße 3, 257 59 807. 2.30 pm–6.30 pm, Tue–Fri; 10 am–2 pm, Sat. Second Nothelfer gallery for Tachism, informel, gestural and narrative painting. *U* to Nollendorfplatz **Map p. 68, 3C**

Galerie Eva Poll Lützowplatz 7, 261 70 91, www.poll-berlin.de. 2 pm–8 pm, Tue–Fri; 4 pm–8 pm, Sat. Critical realism and figurative art of the 1960s, focusing on East German and Russian artists. *U* to Nollendorfplatz **Map p. 68, 3C**

eat

CAFÉS AND RESTAURANTS

€   **Bendig** Potsdamer Platz Arkaden (basement), Alte Potsdamer Straße 7, 379 398 67. *Fleischerei* and canteen with good German fare, from *wurst* and *kartoffelslat* to substantial meat-and-two-veg portions. A seating area and bar provide some shelter from the shopping tumult going on around you. **Map p. 69, 2C**

Cornwall Pastry Co. Beisheim Centre, Auguste-Hauschner Str. 1, 26 93 08 11. 8 am–8 pm, Mon–Fri; 10 am–8 pm, Sat–Sun. Cornish pasties better even than in Cornwall! Beef and Stilton, Mediterranean, Apple and Blackcurrant, all under €4. Tucked away behind the Ritz. *U* to Potsdamerplatz **Map p. 69, 2C**

Salomon Bagels Potsdamer Platz Arkaden (mezzanine), Alte Potsdamer Straße 7, 25 29 76 26. The best bagels in Berlin, so American locals maintain. *U* to Potsdamer Platz **Map p. 69, 2C**

Sushi Circle Potsdamer Platz Arkaden (basement), Alte Potsdamer Straße 7, 25 89 93 98, www.sushi.de. Keiten Sushi on a conveyor belt. Lunch specials for €6.95 including miso soup and green tea. Also sushi to take away. **Map p. 69, 2C**

€€ **Dachgartenrestaurant im Deutschen Bundestag** Platz der Republik 1, 22 62 99 33, www.feinkost-kaefer.de. Surely Berlin's most uniquely-placed restaurant, in the Bundestag itself. Breakfast until 11, then snacks, lunch à la carte, coffee and cakes and classy Neue Deutsche Küche until 12 am. Booking advisable. *S* to Unter den Linden **Map p. 69, 2B**

Desbrosses Potsdamer Platz 3, entrance on Bellevuestraße, 337 776 340, www.desbrosses.com. Open 6.30 am–12 am. Convincing reconstruction of a 19th-C brasserie, attached to the Ritz. A good menu of French and international cuisine, including an impressive lobster counter and an upmarket wine list. **Map p. 69, 2C**

Menardie Restaurant and Beergarden Friederich-List-Ufer, 394 405 10, www.menardie.de. Open 11 am–12 am. Smart biergarten overlooking the Kanzleramt, with a barbeque and a restaurant with Mediterranean cuisine. Uncrowded, with lots of shade under big old chestnut trees. The prices are a little high but the location is unbeatable. **Map p. 69, 1A**

Café am Neuen See Lichtensteinallee 2, 254 49 30. Berlin's most picturesque biergarten in the Tiergarten, on the shores of a boating lake. In the summer it's the place for well-heeled Wessis to be seen. *Wurst*, *Leberkäse* (meatloaf) and pizza are available self-serve, while the restaurant has a good Mediterranean selection. On a warm summer's evening positively paradise. *S* to Unter den Linden, *U* to Potsdamer Platz **Map p. 69, 2C**

BARS

Billy Wilder's Potsdamer Straße. 2, 26 55 48 60, www.billywilders.de. 10 am–2 am (in summer from 6 pm). A certain movie-business glamour seems to rub off on the guests of this permanently busy café/bar. A good place for a coffee or post-film drink. Cocktails €5 during happy hour and 'blue hour'. **Map p. 69, 2C**

Kumpel Nest 3000 Lützowstraße 23, 261 69 18. 5 pm–5 am, Sun–Thur; Fri and Sat the party continues round the clock. This bar is an institution on the Tiergarten party circuit, where anyone can drink and dance until dawn. **Map p. 69, 1C**

Victoria Bar Potsdamer Straße 102, 25 75 99 77, www.victoriabar.de. A short walk from the Kulturforum brings you to the source of some of the best cocktails in town. This smart but easy-going bar is easy to miss. Pass through the thick felt curtains into the dim interior, walk to the big, long bar past op-art murals...this is lounge heaven. Happy hour daily. **U** to Kurfürstenstraße **Map p. 69, 1C**

shop

Flöhmarkt am Tiergarten Straße 17 Juni. 10 am–5 pm, Sat–Sun. Antiques, furniture, clothing, CDs and records, books, film memorabilia, postcards...and a *wurst* stand. Berlin's most-visited flea market is busy in all weather. It's not the cheapest market, though the quality is generally high. Near to the Tiergarten if you need to escape the crowd. **S** to Tiergarten **Map p. 69, B1**

Sony Style Store Alte Potsdamer Straße 4 (entrance in the Sony Centre), 25 75 11 88, www.sony.de. 10 am–8 pm, Mon–Fri; 10 am–4 pm, Sat. The Sony Centre is the mega-corp's European HQ; the four-floor Sony Style Store stocks the complete range of products, from alarm clocks to high-end plasma TVs, and, of course, laptops, laptops, laptops. The store's more like a museum of contemporary consumer technology with exhibits that can be discovered, used, and played with. If you want to buy you order at the counter, though the majority of people come just to ogle. Gadgetry so cutting edge that by the time you've reached the fourth floor what's on the first is out of date. **Map p. 69, 2C**

CHARLOTTENBURG

1　**2**　**3**

MOABIT

Turmstr.

Warmsenstr.　Burgenhagenstr.

Bandelstr.

Lübecker str.

Mathilde-Jacob-Pl.　Ⓤ Turmstr.　Turmstr.

Hütten str.

Erasmus-str.

Allee

Zwinglistr.

Kleiner-Tiergarten

Alt-Moabit

Alt-Moabit

Ottopl.

Alt-Moabit

Pascal-str.

Heisenberg-str.

Morse-str.

Haller-str.

Helmholtzstr.

Zinzendorf str.

Levetzowstr.

Elberfelder-str.

Bochumer str.

Essener str.

Kreuselerstr.

Stromstr.

Claudiusstr.

Kirchstr.

Helgoländer str.

Thomasiusstr.

A

HANSA-VIERTEL

Dortmunder-str.

Flensburgerstr.

Ⓢ Bellevue

Dovestr.

Franklinstr.

Agricola-str.

Tile-Wardenberg-str.

Solinger str.

Hansaufer

Lessing str.

Bartning-

Salz-

Einstein-

Guericke str.

Abbe-str.

hofer str.

Marchstr.

Landwehrkanal

Wullenweberstr.

Schleswiger-ufer

Bachstr.

Ⓤ Hansapl.

Hansapl.　Altonaerstr.

Schlossp.

Bellevu

Grosse

Gutenberg-str.

Englischestr.

Siegmunds Hof

Klopstockstr.

Händelallee

Faulersee O.-Schumann-Pl.

B

Grosse

Stern

Siegessäule

ufer

Tiergarten Ⓢ J.-Haydn-Pl.

Strasse des 17 Juni

Ernst-Reuter-Pl.

Ⓤ Ernst-Reuter-pl.

Hardenbergstr.

Müller-Breslau-Str.

Fasanenstr.

Hertzallee

Neuersee

Goethestr.　Steinpl.

Museum for Fotografie

Hardenbergpl.

Savigny-pl.

Kantstr.

Ⓢ Zoologischer Garten

Bahnhof Zoo

Zoological Garden

Cornelius str.

Stüler str.

Knesebeck str.

Carmerstr.

Beate-Uhse Erotikmus.

Ⓤ Zoologischer Garten

Aquarium

Budapester str.

Kunstforum der Berliner Volksbank

Savigny-pl.

Ⓢ

K.-Wilhelm-Gedächtnis Kirche

Breitscheidpl.

O.-Palme-Pl.

C

Grolmanstr.

Uhlandstr.

Kurfürsten-damm

Kurfürstendamm

Taufentzienstr.

Kurfürsten-

Keithstr.

An der Urania

Joachimstaler pl.

Los-Angeles-Pl.

Augsburger-str.

Ⓤ Wittenbergpl.

Wittenbergpl.

Meinekestr.

Joachimstaler str.

The Story of Berlin

Käthe Kollwitz Museum

Ranke-str.

Augsburger-str.

Nürnberger str.

Lietzen-

Passauer str.

Kleiststr.

Noller-

105

Schloss Charlottenburg

OPEN	*Altes Schloss*: Closed Mon; open 9 am–5 pm, Tue–Fri; 10 am–5 pm, Sat–Sun; *Neue Flügel*: Closed Mon; open 10 am–6 pm, Tue–Fri; 11 am–6 pm; *Neuer Pavillon*: Closed Mon; open 10 am–5 pm, Tue–Fri (last admittance 4.30 pm); *Belvedere*: Closed Mon. Apr 1–Oct 31, 10 am–5 pm, Tue–Sun (last admittance 4.30 pm); Nov 1–Mar 31, 12 am–4 pm,Tue–Fri; 12 pm–5 pm, Sat–Sun (last admittance 4.30 pm); *Mausoleum*: closed Mon, open Apr 1–Oct 31, 10 am–5 pm, Tue–Sun
CHARGES	*Altes Schloss*: €8/€5 *Neue Flügel*: €5/€4 *Neuer Pavillon*: €2/€1.50 *Belvedere*: €2/€1.50 *Mausoleum*: €1/free *Two-day ticket*: €12/€9 (valid for all other buildings in the SPSG, except Potsdam Sanssouci) *Kombi-Karte*: €7/€5 (valid for all areas of the Schloss except the guided tour of the Altes Schloss) Day ticket for Charlottenburg also covers Ägyptisches Museum, Helmut Newton Foundation, Museum for Pre- and Early History, Reproduction Workshops *Family Ticket*: €20 (up to two adults and three children, valid for one month, includes all buildings in the SPSG except Potsdam Sanssouci)
MAIN ENTRANCE	Luisenplatz, Spandauerdamm
U-BAHN	U2 to Sophie-Charlotten-Platz, U7 to Richard-Wagner-Platz
S-BAHN	S45/46 Westend
TELEPHONE	32 09 14 40
WEB	www.spsg.de
SERVICES	There is a shop in the east wing of the courtyard and a café in the former orangerie on the west side, serving traditional German cuisine and an excellent selection of cakes.

HIGHLIGHTS

Crown Prince's Silver	*Room 235*
The Porcelain Cabinet	*Room 95*
The Golden Gallery	*Room 363*
Watteau's *Shop Sign of the Art Dealer Gersaint*	*Room 364*
Tomb of Kaiserin Augusta	*Mausoleum*
Königliche Porzellan Manufaktur	*Belvedere*
Friedrich´s *Morning in the Riesengebirge*	*Pavilion*

HISTORY OF THE SCHLOSS

Between 1695 and 1699, the central part of the palace (the Altes Schloss) was built near the town of Lietzow, west of Berlin. Designed by Arnold Nering, it was intended as a country retreat for Sophie Charlotte, second wife of Friedrich III of Brandenburg and a woman notable in her time for her interest in, and patronage of, the sciences and philosophy (with her mother, Sophie, she was a student of Gottfried Wilhelm Leibniz).

In 1701, the king, now Friedrich I of Prussia, commissioned the Swedish architect Johan Friedrich Eosander to build the wings, courtyard and garden. Friedrich renamed the palace in honour of the 'philosopher queen' after her death in 1705 at the age of 37. The grounds, begun in 1697, were designed in imitation of Versailles. A long approach, now Schloßstraße, extended through the dome to the north of the building and ended in a gondoliering lake.

The palace was expanded in the 18th C under Friedrich the Great, who commissioned Georg Wenzeslaus Knobelsdorff to build a new wing (die neue Flügel). The interior, which included the legendary Golden Gallery, represented the apotheosis of the Frederican Rococo.

During the reign of Friedrich Wilhelm II, Friedrich the Great's nephew, the arts blossomed. He commissioned Carl Gottfried

Schloss Charlottenburg

Langhans to build the Belvedere and Palace Theatre, converted the winter chambers on the upper floor of the new wing and had the garden landscaped in the English style.

After World War I and the collapse of the Prussian ruling house all palaces were transferred to the state and opened to the public in 1927. In World War II the palace was destroyed by fire. Reconstruction work began in the 1950s, restoring only that which could be guaranteed accurate by historical records.

ALTES SCHLOSS

UPPER FLOOR

The upper floor was originally the living quarters of Crown Prince Friedrich Wilhelm I, but was completely remodelled for King Friedrich Wilhelm IV and Queen Elisabeth in 1842. The décor was largely destroyed during World War II and the rooms now contain objects from the Royal couple's Charlottenburg apartments with other items from apartments in Berlin and Potsdam.

The **Crown Prince's Silver** on display in *Room* 235 was a gift from 414 Prussian cities to celebrate the engagement of the Prussian Crown Prince Wilhelm and Princess Cecilie in 1904. Production was interrupted by World War I and the set never came into the possession of the Royal Family. It was taken to the US at the end of the war and returned at the request of Chancellor Ernst Reuter in 1949.

The 2,964-piece set was designed by Ignatius Taschner and Emil Lettré, among others, in a mix of Neo-Classicism and Jugendstil. The bombastic end pieces—Indian and African Elephants carrying obelisks—were designed by August Gaul, the most famous animal sculptor of the time.

Room 234 has a silver ornamental goblet to commemorate the 'The Enchantment of the White Rose', a festival in 1829 marking the birthday and wedding anniversary of Princess Charlotte von Preußen, or Kaiserin Alexandra Feodorowna, as she was called after her marriage to Tsar Nikolaus I. The festival included a reconstruction of medieval knightly games and classically themed *tableaux vivants* designed by Schinkel. The goblet itself, also by

SCHLOSS CHARLOTTENBURG

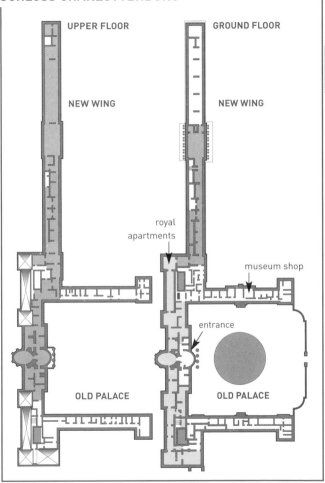

UPPER FLOOR

GROUND FLOOR

NEW WING

NEW WING

royal
apartments

museum shop

entrance

OLD PALACE

OLD PALACE

Schinkel, together with the court silversmith Hossauer, is one of three versions. This one belonged to the state of Mecklenburg until 1986 and was bought on the art market in 1996. A second went missing after the war and a third is in St. Petersburg.

The **Crown Cabinet** (*Kronkabinett*) *(Room 236)* contains all that remains of the Hohenzollern crown jewels. These include the electoral sword donated by Pope Pious II in 1460 in acknowledgement of participation in the Crusades; the gold frames of the crowns worn by Friedrich I and Sophie Charlotte; and the jewel and the chain of the Order of the Black Eagle, the highest honour of state. The engravings show the ceremonial procession at the coronation of Friedrich I in Königsberg in 1701.

The **Green Room** *(Room 212)* typifies the taste of mid-19th-C royal interior design, with Biedermeier genre paintings, Italian landscapes and bouquet still lives. See *Voltaire Dressing* (c.1850), a small work by the prolific **Adolph Menzel.**

Important paintings in the **Study Room** *(Room 204)* reflect the Romantic tastes of Friedrich Wilhelm IV, patron of major early 19th-C artists. They include *The Gulf of La Spezia* and *Nine Sketches from the Trip to Italy* (1828/29) by **Carl Blechen**, *View of a Harbour* by **Caspar David Friedrich** (1815/16), and *Triumphal Arch* by **Karl Schinkel** (1817). Works by all three artists can be seen more extensively in the Alte Nationalgalerie (see p. 28).

GROUND FLOOR

The royal apartments of the ground floor can only be viewed in guided tours, in German (there's a leaflet in English). They run every forty-five minutes from the doorway next to the ticket counter.

The **Porcelain Cabinet** *(in Room 95)* is the highlight of the tour. The current collection, put together from the art market and dating predominantly from the K'ang-hsi period (1662–1722), replaces the original collection, decimated during World War II. The original porcelain collection was installed to reflect the new prestige of Friedrich I, and reflected the 18th-C vogue for all things Chinese.

THE NEW WING

The upper floor of the New Wing suffered serious war damage and has been extensively reconstructed. At the top of the stairs, on the east, or left hand side, are the White Hall and the **Golden Gallery**, masterpieces of Friderician Rococo completely reconstructed between 1961 and 1973 from photographic records. They are followed by the Second Apartment of Friedrich the Great, which contains a number of interesting artworks. On the west side is the First Apartment of Friedrich the Great and the Winter Chambers of Frederick William II.

The **Concert Room** *(Room 364)* has the celebrated painting *Shop Sign of the Art Dealer Gersaint* by **Antoine Watteau** (1721). It was intended as an advertisement for Gersaint's gallery. The dealer put it on the market, where it was bought by Friedrich in 1744.

Watteau's caricatures of ennui, narcissism, prurience and connoisseurship are an ironic commentary on the art-buying public of the time. On the left a portrait of Ludwig XIV is being packed away: this plays on the name of the gallery, *'Au grand monarque'*, and alludes to the outdated style of painting produced under the king. To one side a cavalier beckons a lady into the shop, which opens to the street, creating a staged impression. On the right, two customers look into a mirror, a luxury object also sold by art dealers. Further back, a man kneels to inspect a nude, while his companion inspects the brushwork with a magnifying glass.

On the **ground floor** of the New Wing, in *Room 123*, is a model of the Berlin Stadtschloss (City Palace), former residence of the Hohenzollerns, opposite the Museumsinsel. The Palace was badly damaged by wartime bombing and demolished by the Communist authorities in 1950. Planning permission has been granted to rebuild the façade on the original site, though state funding has been ruled out; no one knows for sure when work is due to begin.

A walk through the park brings you to the **Mausoleum**, the burial place of the Hohenzollerns, built in 1810 in the style of a Doric temple and extended in 1841 and 1888-90. Inside are the tomb statues of King Friedrich Wilhelm III, Kaiser Wilhelm I and Kaiserin Augusta. The black marble and the Jugendstil candlestick holders lend the mausoleum a *fin de siècle* theatricality.

Following the path round through the modern part of the park, you come to the **Belvedere**. This miniature palace was commissioned by Friedrich Wilhelm II and built by Carl Langhans in 1788. After sustaining severe wartime damage, the exterior was rebuilt and the floor plan restored on the second and first floors. The Belvedere holds the **Brandenburg state porcelain**, a collection of the highest quality, with an emphasis on Königliche Porzellan Manufaktur (KPM). Previously, porcelain had been used for dessert only, since—unlike silver—its surface was not eroded by fruity acids. In the mid-18th C it began to be used for larger dishes, as well as cups and saucers to provide for the vogue for the new hot drinks: tea, coffee and chocolate.

Walking back up the eastern edge of the garden towards the palace brings you to the **New Pavilion**. Friedrich Wilhelm III intended the Italian-style villa, built by Karl Friedrich Schinkel in 1825/5, as a retreat for himself and his second wife Auguste von Liegnitz. After the king's death in 1840, it was used as a museum and library. The restored pavilion (the interior was burned during World War II) houses a collection of art from the Schinkel period, including paintings by Schinkel himself, **Caspar David Friedrich**, **Carl Blechen** and **Eduard Gaertner**, alongside furniture, porcelain and jewellery.

Friedrich's *Morgen in Riesengebirge* (c.1811) in Room 23 is one of the artist's most famous images. Completed from sketches made in the Erzgebirge mountain range east of Dresden, it sets the dramatic landscape alongside the symbolism of the resurrection (the sunrise) and the figure of faith (the woman in white) pulling the artist up to her.

Of the architectural paintings by Eduard Gaertner, *Panorama of Berlin from the Roof of the Friedrichwerdeschen Church in Six Parts* (1834) is the most spectacular. The incorporation of the roof of the church increases the viewer's illusion of involvement in the scene and enables orientation. In the southern section, Schinkel, the architect of the church, can be seen in a top hat. The cupolas of the German and French Cathedrals, the spire of the Nikolai Church, and the roof of the Stadtschloß rise over the rooftops. In the northern section you see, from the left, the cupola of the

Hedwigskirche, the Opera House, the Kronprinzenpalais, the Alte Museum and the Berlin Cathedral. Gaertner was the most significant German architectural painter of the century and this painting was displayed, on a hinged frame, in Friedrich Wilhelm III's apartment. However the increasing preference for the grandiose rendered Gaertner's urbane style obsolete, and the painter was neglected later in his career.

MUSEUM OF PRE- AND EARLY HISTORY

This museum, in the Langhans Building, has an exceptional collection of artifacts from Europe and the Ancient Near East, from the Stone Age through the Neolithic and Bronze Ages to the Early Middle Ages. Especially interesting are exhibits on the development of agricultural societies in the Near East, the collection of ceramics from the Caucasus and Mesopotamia, and gold, ceramics and weaponry found at the site of Troy in 1870.

Museum Berggruen

PICASSO AND HIS TIME

OPEN	The museum is open 10 am–6 pm, Tue–Sun.
CLOSED	Mon
CHARGES	€6/€3 (includes audio guide). Entry free on Thur after 2 pm (without audio guide). No charge for children up to 16 years. Day ticket to all SMPK museums €10/€5; three day ticket to all SMPK museums €12/€6.
MAIN ENTRANCE	Schloss Straße 1
U-BAHN	U to Sophie-Charlotten-Platz or Richard-Wagner-Platz
S – BAHN	S45/46 Westend
TELEPHONE	32 69 58 15
WEB	www.smb.spk-berlin.de
SERVICES	A small but well-stocked shop, no café.

HIGHLIGHTS

Pablo Picasso's *Seated Harlequin* (1905),
Bottle, Absinthe Glass, Books, Pipe, Violin, Clarinet Resting on a Piano (1911-12),
Yellow Pullover (1939) and
Matador and Nude (1970)

Paul Klee's *Room Perspective With Dark Door* (1921) and
Versiegelte Dame (Sealed Lady) (1930)

Alberto Giacometti's *Square* (1948–49)

HEINZ BERGGRUEN AND HIS COLLECTION

Heinz Berggruen was born in Berlin in 1914 into a Jewish trading family. He began his career as a journalist for the *Frankfurter Allegemeine Zeitung*, and in 1936 emigrated to the United States with a scholarship to Berkeley. After the war he returned to Germany as a GI, where he was put in charge of publishing an arts magazine, part of the allied attempt to reinstill democratic values into the defeated nation. Delegated to Paris with UNESCO, he established a gallery near the D'Orsay in 1947.

Berggruen became associated with **Pablo Picasso** when he exhibited drawings from the collection of American author Gertrude Stein. **Paul Klee** formed a counter pole to Picasso for Berggruen from the beginning; *Perspektive Ghost* (1939), now in the New York Metropolitan, was Berggruen's first acquisition, bought from a New York second-hand dealer for $100. **Cézanne**, **Seurat** and **Van Gogh** were later additions to the collection; **Matisse**, whose paper cut-outs Berggruen exhibited in the 1950s, was given up in order to avoid an imbalance. Before moving to Berlin, the collection hung alongside the old masters in the National Gallery in London, where some works, including a Seurat study, have remained.

Alongside his career as a collector, Berggruen has published novels and short stories. A regular figure in Berlin public life, he was made an honorary citizen of the city in 2004. Heinz Berggruen has been known to mingle with the visitors to the museum: should a white-haired man appear beside you and begin talking about a painting, take note!

THE COLLECTION

The tour of the museum begins on the ground floor and goes in an anticlockwise direction.

The first thing we come to are paintings and collages by **Matisse**. *The Blue Portfolio* (1945) is striking for its deep, sensual red against the blue of the portfolio and dress: here Matisse was developing his technique of contrasting colour fields. Notice the impressive leopard skin on the wall. *Woman Skipping Rope* (1952) is one of what Matisse called his 'paintings with scissors'; close inspection reveals pin holes in the guache-painted shapes where he experimented with the composition. The figure is positioned to the right, creating tension, and the overall effect is one of arrested movement. The next room has graphic work by Matisse, including a poster design for an exhibition at the Tate.

The third room has two works from **Picasso**'s 'Blue Period', of which *Portrait of Jaime Sabartés* (1904) is a prime example: the man's lugubrious gaze and ironic smile fascinates. Sabartés was a writer who frequented Picasso's locale; there was a meeting of minds and the two men corresponded daily. Picasso began the portrait after an unsatisfactory evening in the café and finished it by the morning, by which time his bad mood had been absorbed into the painting. Returning from South America after thirty years, Sabartés became Picasso's private secretary, organising studio visits to the now world-famous artist, and, as a mistress of Picasso observed sourly, serving as his private whipping-boy.

Sabartés' ruddy lips also herald Picasso's 'Pink Period', represented in this room by *Seated Harlequin* (1905). The study, inspired by the visit of a troupe of acrobats to Montmartre, was one of several similar portraits which ended in the monumental *Les Saltimbanques*. The next room has examples of studies from a period of high productivity, including wood prints, still lifes, and linear studies, of which the finest is *Head of a Woman* (1906–67), thought to have been influenced by ancient Iberian statues exhibited in the Louvre in 1906.

The final room on the ground floor has **African sculpture**. Little is known for sure about the Ijo Figures from Nigeria: they may represent forest spirits or heroes. Their two-faced heads suggest watchfulness, while the medicine bags on their arms and torso suggest wisdom or strength. The appearance of teeth during childhood was seen as a sign of providence: in sculpture, the spirit took possession of the form as soon as the teeth had been carved. The 18th-C *Memorial Head* from Nigeria was likely modelled from the severed head of a defeated rebel and sent back to his tribe as a warning. The neck rings are a feature of the Oba tribe: they would have been pearl, and would have had magic properties; pearls are also attached to the cap and ears. The opening at the top of the cap was for a carved elephant tusk. The room is dominated by the *Large Bird* (19th- or 20th-C) from the Senufo people of the Ivory Coast, renowned for their abilities in wood carving. This bird, the Abyssinian ground hornbill, was sacred, and would have presided over the ceremonial elevation of young men into the tribal hierarchy. The holes in the wings were in order to secure the carving during festive dancing.

Picasso saw African art of this kind at the Musée de Trocadero. His *Study for Demoiselles d'Avignon* (1907) reworks earlier, more Classically-influenced designs towards the mask-like features that would appear in the final version. It is the first time distortion appeared in his work.

Alberto Giacometti's sculpture *Standing Woman* (1960) is in the hallway. Giacometti's bronzes were often made from the same clay figure—he worked and reworked, making a cast each time a sculptural form was reached.

The first room on the first floor shows paintings in the Analytic Cubist style. Picasso's *Bottle, Absinthe Glass, Books, Pipe, Violin, Clarinet resting on a Piano* (1911–12) confuses the eye with spatial inconsistencies and incompletely described objects, which begin to cohere only after a long look. The painting was one of a series commissioned by a Brooklyn art collector, who sent Picasso a sketch of the wall measurements of his library, which explains the unusual shape of the canvas.

The second room has smaller cubist studies by Picasso and images of corpulent nudes in a parody of classical Greek and Roman statues. In the next room, *Portrait of a Woman* (1923), created during a summer holiday in the Antibes, is made entirely of sand. The next room contains smaller studies, including the simple but ambivalent *Couple* (1927).

The fifth room on the first floor contains a number of impressive paintings, including portraits of Dora Maar, Picasso's mistress and subject of numerous portraits. Picasso first spied Dora in the Café des Deux Magots in Paris: she was jabbing a knife into the table through the spaces between her fingers. When she brought her hand up, it was bleeding—apparently from that moment on Picasso was hooked. A later mistress described Maar's strange immobility: this quality comes through in *Yellow Pullover* (1939). The item of clothing resembles coiled rope, as if she was bound to her chair. Notice her left hand, too, tensed and gnarled. *Dora Maar with Green Fingernails* (1936) again shows Picasso's fascination with her hands: here they are sharp and tipped with green.

Large Reclining Nude (1942) is a war painting in mood, if not in subject matter. Picassos' wartime seclusion is reflected in this claustrophobic, tortured painting of Dora Maar; Heinz Berggruen has called this Picasso's bitterest painting.

The next room contains studies completed around the period of *Guernica* (1937), Picasso's depiction of the chaos and suffering of the Spanish Civil War. As in the masterpiece, bulls and horses have a central role in *Minotauromachie* (1935). *Seated Woman* (1940) is a more playful work created out of objects, including torn cigarette boxes, lying around Picasso's studio.

The final room on the first floor leaves the wartime era and represents Picasso's later oeuvre. *The Reading* (1953) is a portrait of Françoise Gilot, a mistress who left Picasso in the same year. *Portrait of a Young Woman After Cranach* (1958) was inspired by a postcard of the 16th-C German painter's *Portrait of a Noblewoman* (1564). The woman in Cranach's original has a cool half smile, which Picasso brought to his version, along with the black curtain and looming shadows behind. Nevertheless, Picasso jokily abandoned Cranach's delicate tonality for bright, blocked marks. Brighter still is *Matador and Nude* (1970), one of around two hundred paintings Picasso produced in his nineties, all apparently half finished: here, the pale of the nude's skin is blank canvas. Picasso's furious work rate was an attempt, he said, to attain immediacy, the perfect form.

The second floor is given over to works by Paul Klee, Berggruen's greatest passion after Picasso. *Room Perspective With Dark Door* (1921) was one of a number of tracings from an original study Klee made while serving in the army; full of indefinable technical instruments, the room could be a laboratory or operating theatre.

In 1921 Klee received a professorial post at the Bauhaus, where he taught in the glass worshop: the new geometric style is evident in *Architecture of Planes* (1923), as is his concern with transparency. The grid-like structure allows colour gradations to take place as if in a colour chart: composition is restrained, though an overly mechanical effect is avoided via the hand-drawn lines. Like in *Room Perspective*, the central form is illuminated against a dark ground, a technique often interpreted in metaphysical terms.

In 1931 Klee left the Bauhaus and moved to the Academy of Arts in Düsseldorf. His work from this period marks a departure from an interest in the way space is formed by colour and light to concern with surfaces and 'polyphony': *Classical Coast* (1931), influenced by mosaics Klee saw in Ravenna, is made of horizontal rows of points.

Also in this room is Giacometti's *Square* (1948–9), which conveys with minimal means the anonymity of city dwellers. Giacometti said in 1961, that 'rather like ants, each appears as if he moves completely alone, in a direction the others don't know. They meet, they pass. Without looking at one another. Or they move around a motionless woman. It ocurred to me that I am able only to represent a motionless woman and a moving man.'

Works by Klee from the mid-1920s in the next room have a distinctly surreal touch. *Chinese Porcelain* (1923) is a peculiar medley of Chinese erotic porcelain and Christian devotionalia, while *Study at Breakfast* (1925) is an early-morning meditation on creation. In language, as in art, Klee tended towards understatement. *Sealed Lady* (1930) shows a woman styled urbanely, with boyish coiffeur, pale makeup, her silence sealed by red-painted lips. *The Sparse Words of the Frugal*, in which only the consonants of the title have been included, has a Zen-like, aphoristic quality.

Works produced when Klee was suffering terminal illness have a predominance of black. *The Carpet* (1940—the year Klee died) places heavy bars between the viewer and the world of colour. On his grave were to be the words: 'I am living amongst the dead and the unborn, one step closer to creation, but nowhere near enough.'

in the area

CHARLOTTENBURG

Bröhan museum Schloßstraße 1a, 32 69 06 00, www.broehan-museum.de. 10 am–6 pm, Tue–Sat. Behind the Museum Berggruen is the state museum for Art Nouveau, Art Deco and Functionalism from 1889–1939. The collection includes painting and sculpture as well as the applied arts. Artists include Emile Gallé, Hector Guimard, Peter Behrens, Hanry van de Velde and Josef Hoffmann. **U** to Sophie-Charlotten-Platz/Richard-Wagner Platz **Map p. 104, 2B**

Beate-Uhse Erotikmuseum Joachimstaler Straße 4, 10 62 3, www.erotikmuseum.de. 9 am–12 am. Located above the sex shop chain founded by former Luftwaffe pilot and liberator of postwar mores Beate Uhse. The prints, pricks and paraphernalia behind glass seem positively staid in the light of the activities on the ground floor. **U** to Zoologischer Garten **Map p. 105, 2C**

Egyptian Museum and Papyrus Collection Schloßstraße 70, 34 35 73 11, www.smpk.de. 10 am–6 pm, Tue–Sun. Extremely comprehensive and well-laid out museum with a range of fascinating and beautiful exhibits, from pencils and pipe cleaners to priestesses with bulbous crania. Nefertiti steals the show, however. Found in Armana in 1913 by Gustave Lefebvre, the three-thousand-year-old bust captivates through its symmetry and aqualine elegance. *U* to Sophie-Charlotten-Platz/Richard-Wagner Platz **Map p. 104, 2B**

Gipsformere Sophie-Charlotten-Straße 17–18, 32 67 69 11, www.smpk.de. 9 am–4 pm, Mon–Tue and Thur–Fri; until 6 pm on Wed. Get your very own bust of Nefertiti, Goethe or Julius Caesar. The Replica Workshop has been collecting molds since 1819, and owns a collection on a par with the Louvre and the British Museum. Founded to give the public as wide an access as possible to works of antiquity, it now provides garden sculptures to wealthy Munich businessmen. Visit the showroom or take a tour around the workshops (1st Wed of the month, 10 am). *U* to Sophie-Charlotten-Platz, *S* to Westend **Map p. 104, 1A**

Museum für Fotografie/Helmut Newton Foundation Jebenstraße 2, www.smb.spk.berlin.de. 10 am–6 pm, Tue–Sat. Just before his death, Newton made a permanent loan of 1,000 photographs to the city he was forced to leave in 1938. These are now exhibited in the former Gallery of the 20th C, along with works by his wife Alice Springs, including pictures of her husband after his death. The Newton bequest is in rotation along with works by other photographers. *U* to Zoologischer Garten **Map p. 105, 2C**

Käthe Kollwitz Museum Fasanenstraße 24, 882 52 10. 11 am–6 pm, Wed–Mon, www.kaethe-kollwitz.de. Käthe Kollwitz was Berlin's leading woman artist during the 1920s and 1930s. Her Expressionist style did not please the Nazis; later her husband was murdered in a camp in 1940. She died in Moritzburg near Dresden at the end of the war. This museum shows her sculpture, drawings and prints. *U* to Uhlandstraße **Map p. 105, 1C**

Kaiser-Wilhelm-Gedächtnis Kirche Bretscheidplatz, 218 5023, www.gedaechtniskirche.com. 10 am–4 pm, Mon–Sat. West Berlin's most postcarded sight is a 19th-C church destroyed by bombing in 1943 and left in ruins as a reminder of the damage inflicted upon the city. The modern Gedenkhalle (hall of remembrance) has stained blue glass tiles that create an ethereal glow when seen from within. *U* to Zoologischer Garten **Map p. 105, 2C**

The Story of Berlin Kurfürstendamm 207–8, 887 20 100, www.story-of-berlin.de. 10 am–8 pm, last tour of the bunker at 6 pm. Believe it or not, below the Ku'damm is a nuclear bomb shelter, built in the early 1970s to hold around 3,500 people. It can be visited as part of this excellent

Gas masks at The Story of Berlin

exhibition of the city's history, covering its foundation in 1237, its expansion through the ages, the fall of the empire and the Golden Twenties, National Socialism and wartime destruction, Cold War division, the fall of the wall and beyond. Audio guides in English are available. *U* to Kurfürstendamm **Map p. 105, 1C**

Zoo and Aquarium Hardenbergplatz 8, 254 010. 9 am–5 pm. The zoo, positioned directly in the city centre, was built in 1841, but had to be almost entirely rebuilt after the war. With approximately 14,000 animals, it is huge; the aquarium is particularly beautiful. *U* to Zoologischer Garten **Map p. 105, 3C**

FURTHER AFIELD

Brücke Museum Bussardsteig 9, 831 2029. 11 am–5 pm, closed Tue, admission €4. Devoted to the untamed forms and vibrant colours of Ernst Ludwig Kirchner, Karl Schmidt-Rottluff, Max Pechstein, Emil Nolde, Otto Mueller, and **Erich Heckler** (see picture on p. 123), all part of the radical early 20th-C art circle called *Die Brücke* ('The Bridge'). The

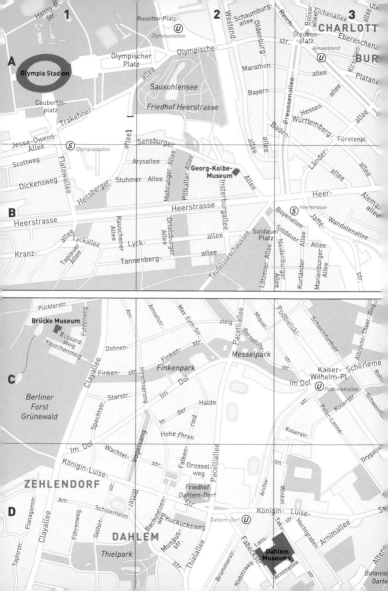

Erich Heckler *Fränzi liegend* (1910) at the Brücke Museum

museum is an Expressionist gem perched on the edge of the Grunewald Forest, and worth the trek. Bus 115 to Pücklerstraße **Map p. 122, 1C**

Dahlem Museums (Museum of Indian Art, Museum of East Asian Art, Museum of Ethnology and the Museum of European Cultures) Lansstraße 8, 830 1361. 10 am–6 pm, Tue–Fri; 11 am–6 pm, Sat and Sun. Several collections housed under one roof. The South and East Asian galleries are particularly noteworthy for their Ghandaran and Mathuran stone sculptures and Chinese and Japanese calligraphy and woodblocks. The newly designed exhibition spaces are innovative, displaying objects in niches that mimic their original surroundings and including an interactive computer program that narrates the life of the Buddha. *U* to Dahlem Dorf **Map p. 122, 2D**

Georg-Kolbe-Museum Sensburger Allee 25, 304 21 44, www.georg-kolbe-museum. 10 am–5 pm, Tue–Sun. Georg Kolbe was Germany's leading sculptor during the in the first half of the 20th C. Specialising in nudes, he toyed with Expressionism before World War I but returned to undistorted representation during the Weimar era. His muscular figures were exploited by the Nazis, and though the artist declined to portray Hitler, he can be said to have been an indirect collaborator. His former studio in this secluded part of Charlottenburg was opened in 1950 as an exhibition space for his work. *S* to Heerstraße **Map p. 122, 2B**

Charlottenburg's Sculpture Boulevard

The Sculpture Boulevard was installed in 1987 to commemorate's Berlin's 750th anniversary. Of the seven sculptures, only three remain. The best-known and most obvious is **Brigitte and Martin Matchinsky-Denninghof**'s *Berlin*, a 9-m steel and chrome knot in the centre of busy Tauentzienstraße, near Marburger Straße. *Pyramid* by **Joseph Erben** is a steel rib secured by two cables, straddling the junction of Kürfürestendamm and Bleibtreustraße. At Rathenauplatz, at the westernmost end of the Kurfürstendamm where it joins the motorway, is **Wolf Vostell**'s *Cadillacs in the Form of the Naked Maja*, two Cadillacs covered in concrete. The sculpture was so unpopular it received bomb threats. Vostell solicited letters railing against the work, which he then dumped, unread, into the concrete mass.

commercial galleries

Aedes West Rosenthaler Straße 40-41, 312 25 98. Forum for experimental, architectural-based work. *S* to Savignyplatz **Map p. 9, 2A**

Galerie Barthel & Tetzner Fasanenstraße 15, 1st floor, 88 68 33 06 07, www.barthel-tetzner.de. Individual and group shows of postwar art, primarily from the former GDR. *U* to Uhlandstraße **Map p. 105, 1C**

Galerie Brockstedt Mommsenstraße 59, 885 05 00, www.galerie brockstedt.de. Classical modernism and contemporary painting and sculpture. *S* to Savignyplatz **Map p. 104, 3C**

Galerie Brusberg Kurfürstendamm 213, 882 76 82/3, www.brusberg-berlin.de. Modernism, Surrealism and contemporary art. *U* to Uhlandstraße **Map 105, 1C**

Camera Work Kantstrasse 149, 31 50 47 83. Photographic archive of over 1.2 million negatives, 25,000 vintage photos and 150,000 originals, with temporary exhibitions. *S* to Savignyplatz **Map p. 105, 1C**

Galerie Horst Dietrich Giesebrechtstraße 19, 324 53 45, www.galerie dietrich.de. Contemporary artists: books, sculpture and photography. *U* to Adenauerplatz **Map p. 104, 3C**

Galerie Thea Fischer Rheinhardt Fasanenstraße 29 (in the walkway), 882 40 57, www.fischer-reinhardt.de. Contemporary painting and sculpture, from abstract to figurative. *U* to Uhlandstraße **Map p. 105, 1C**

Galerie Haas & Fuchs Niebuhrstraße 5, 889 29 190, www.galeriehaasundfuchs.de. Contemporary international painting, photography and sculpture. *S* to Savignyplatz **Map p. 105, 1C**

Kunst & Primitives Pestalozzistraße 100, 313 91 92. Traditional art from Africa and elsewhere. *U* to Ernst-Reuter-Platz, *S* to Savignyplatz **Map p. 105, 1C**

Georg Nothelfer Uhlandstraße 184, 881 44 05. Well-established gallery showing Tachisme, Informel, scriptural, gestural and narrative painting, drawing and sculpture. Artists include Chillida, Hartmann, Serra and Thiele. *U* to Uhlandstraße **Map p. 105, 1C**

Galerie Meinhold & Reucker Giesebrechtstraße 2, 88 70 19 99, www.galerie-meinhold.de. Painting and drawing from the last twenty years. *U* to Adenauerplatz **Map p. 104, 3C**

Galerie Nierendorf Hardenbergstraße 19, 288 772 77. Established gallery showing art of the 20th C. *U* to Zoologischer Garten **Map p. 105, 2C**

Villa Oppenheim Schloßstraße 55, 902 92 4151, www.villaoppenheim.de. Cultural centre near the Schloss Charlottenburg. *U* to Sophie-Charlotten-Platz, *S* to Westend **Map p. 104, 2B**

Galerie Pels-Leusden Fasanenstraße 25, 885 91 50, www.pels-leusden.com. Classical modern (German Impressionism, New Objectivity, Informel) and contemporary: Beckmann, Corinth, Dix, Hartung, Heckel, Kollwitz, Nolde, Ury, Zille. *U* to Uhlandstraße **Map p. 105, 1C**

Art Galerie Richter Kurfürstendamm 188, 883 60 66, www.artgalerie richter.de. International modern art, artists include Hundertwasser and Christo. *U* to Adenauerplatz **Map p. 104, 3C**

Galerie Thomas Schulte Mommsenstraße 56, 32 40 44, www.galerie thomasschulte.de. Post-1960 with a focus on conceptual. Artists include Rebecca Horn, Gordon Matta-Clark and Richard Deacon. *S* to Savignyplatz, *U* to Adenauerplatz **Map p. 104, 3C**

Galerie Michael Schulz Mommsenstraße 34, 324 15 91, www.galerie-schultz.de. Contemporary German and international, with an emphasis on painting and sculpture. *U* to Adenauerplatz **Map p. 104, 3C**

Galerie Springer & Winckler Fasanenstraße 13, 315 72 20, www.springer-winckler.de. Contemporary art of all genres; artists include Appelt, Baselitz, Chillida, Goldsworthy, Lüpertz, Polke and Richter. *U* to Uhlandstraße **Map p. 105, 1C**

Stolz Berlin Goethestraße 81/III, 313 78 99. Viewings by appointment. Constructivism, Russian avant garde, Bauhaus, de Stijl. *U* to Ernst-Reuter-Platz, *S* to Savignyplatz **Map p. 105, 1C**

Galerie Theis Ceramic Neufertstraße 6, 321 23 22. Gallery near the Schloss Charlottenburg showing contemporary ceramics. *U* to Sophie-Charlotten-Platz, *S* to Westend **Map p. 104, 2B**

TVDArt Schlüterstraße 54, corner or Niebuhrstraße, 889 14 445. International art from the 1920s to the 1970s, specialising in the classical modernist movement in Latvia. *S* to Savignyplatz **Map p. 105, 1C**

Kunsthandel Wolfgang Werner Fasanenstraße 72, 882 76 16, www.kunst handel-werner.de. Art of the 19th and 20th centuries, including Nabis, Expressionism, Bauhaus, postwar. *U* to Uhlandstraße **Map p. 105, 1C**

eat

€ **Pizzeria Ali Baba** Bleibtreustraße 45, 881 13 50. 11.30 am–3 pm. Famously good-value Italian restaurant with take-away during the day and a lively and informal restaurant in the evening. The food's fine, and the pasta portions can be ordered small or large, the large only marginally more expensive. Recommended for a cheap and cheerful evening out. *U* to Uhlandstraße, *S* to Savignyplatz **Map p. 105, 1C**

Café Hardenberg Hardenbergstraße 10, 312 33 30. 9 am–1 am, Sun–Thur; 9 am–2 am, Fri–Sat. Spacious Viennese-style coffee house given an academic atmosphere by students from the nearby Technische Universität and Universität der Kunst. Serves breakfast until 5 pm and reasonably priced food until midnight. An ideal place to while away a lazy Sunday engaging in the art of conversation. *U* to Ernst-Reuter-Platz **Map p. 105, 1B**

Galerie Café Reet Klausener Platz 5, 322 48 22. 8 am–7.30, Mon–Fri; 9 am–7.30 pm, Sat–Sun. Light, airy café just down the road from the Schloss, away from the more touristy places. Specialises in the all-day breakfast, also tramezzini, baguettes and cakes. There are lots of magazines to browse if you feel like spending an hour or two resting weary feet. **Map p. 104, B1**

Schwarzes Café Kantstraße 148, 313 80 38. Ask Berliners to name one café in Charlottenburg, this will be it. Open all hours, with a cheap menu. The place to come if you don't want anyone to notice your five-o-clock shadow. **S** to Savignyplatz **Map p. 105, 1C**

Zwiebelfisch Savignyplatz 7/8, 312 73 63, www.zwiebelfisch-berlin.de, 12 pm–6 am, kitchen until 3 am. Back in the 1960s this bar was one of the places to be for the student movement. Now that Savignyplatz has become establishment, Zwiebelfisch is a refuge for unrepentant '68ers, making for a down-to-earth and occasionally raucous atmosphere. Food is cheap and available late. **U** to Uhlandstraße, **S** to Savignyplatz **Map p. 105, 1C**

€€ 31 Bleibtreustraße 31, 884 74 603, www.bleibtreu.com. 7 am–12 am. Chic café and deli at the southern end of Bleibtreustraße doing breakfast sandwiches, wraps, salads and grilled meat, with seating on the pavement or in the attractively designed open-plan interior and courtyard. A good place for lunch after browsing the boutiques. The adjoining restaurant is more upmarket. **Map p. 105, 1C**

Ranke 2 Rankestraße 2, 883 88 82. Traditional German hospitality in the heart of West Berlin—good solid food washed down with beer and schnapps. The waitresses knock on the table before each round, a sure sign of authenticity. Photographs of past chancellors hang on the walls, from Ernst Reuter to Gerhard Schroeder. **U** to Kurfürstendamm **Map p. 105, 2C**

Restaurant Trio Klausenerplatz 14, 321 77 82. 10 am–12 pm. Pleasant, modern restaurant also a short distance from the Schloss, serving all-day breakfast and a lunchtime menu for €10 (main course and dessert). The evening menu begins at 5.30 and has a French emphasis. **Map p. 104, 1B**

€€€Florian Grolmanstraße 52, 313 91 84, www.restaurant-florian.de. 6 pm–3 am. Restaurant famed for its southern German cuisine and popularity with the film industry—during the Berlinale it overflows onto the streets. The menu changes daily but is unfailingly mouthwatering (except perhaps for vegetarians). The interior is unshowy, the tables close together, and atmosphere is informal. Booking advisable. **U** to Uhlandstraße, **S** to Savignyplatz **Map p. 105, 2C**

Marjellchen Mommsenstraße 9, 88 32 676. 5 pm–late (kitchen until 10.30 pm). East-Prussian/Silesian restaurant with a wonderfully traditional feel: dark-stained furniture, walls covered with old still lifes and photos of ageless Schlager stars, and heavy cut-crystal lights. The menu is equally traditional—where else could you order roast leg of elk, stag and boar goulash, Pomeranian goose, or the regional speciality, *Königsburger Klopse*? Booking advisable. *U* to Uhlandstraße, *S* to Savignyplatz **Map p. 105, 1C**

shop

CLOTHES

Bleibgrün Bleibtreustraße 29, 882 16 89, www.bleibgruen.de. Exclusive shoes and upmarket designer fashions for women. Run by the daughter of the owner of Oggi, opposite, an ultra smart shop with designs by Yamamoto and Miyake, where entry is by appointment only. For more information on fashion in Charlottenburg, see www.kurfuerstendamm.de. **Map p. 105, 1C**

Hautnah Uhlandstraße 170, 882 34 34, www.hautnahmode.de. Open afternoons only. As the name ('skin tight') suggests, this shop specialises in fetish gear, mainly for women. Leather and latex get-up, with thigh-length platform boots, corsets, bodices, body suits and more. Also stocks a range of accessories including whips, cuffs, gags, masks... All the items can be tried on in a polite and upfront atmosphere. *U* to Uhlandstraße **Map p. 105, 1C**

Annette Peterson Bleibtreustraße 49, 323 25 56. Long-established West Berlin designer specialising in bold and unconventional clothing for women, designed to be combined with standard gear: wear one of her funky corsets with a pair of jeans and you've got a unique and eyecatching outfit. Peterson also creates accessories, and her customers apparently include women looking for Ascot hats. *U* to Uhlandstraße, *S* to Savignyplatz **Map p. 105, 1C**

Planet Berlin Schlüterstraße 35, 885 27 17. The first stop for rockers: this shop opened nearly twenty years ago when West Berlin wore black and sung along to Nina Hagen. Now Nina Hagen has made a comeback and black rules once again. *U* to Uhlandstraße, *S* to Savignyplatz **Map p. 105, 1C**

Andrea Schelling Gewänder Mommsenstraße 3, 313 21 39,
www.andreaschelling.com. Exquisite hand-made clothing for
women with many one-off pieces. The designs are incredibly
feminine, with layers and folds of diaphanous, shimmering
materials. A classical, faerie queen look is combined with a keen eye
for style and a range of pale, sherbet colours. The owner herself
models her designs, which also include shawls and bags. *U* to
Uhlandstraße, *S* to Savignyplatz **Map p. 105, 1C**

BOOKS AND MUSIC

Germany is the biggest book market in Europe, thanks partly to natural
enthusiasm and partly to tax breaks on so-called '*Kulturgüter*' (a
culturally beneficial product). A bookstore in Germany is something to
see even if you don't read German: the selection is huge, partly due to a
lenient shelf-life policy and partly to the number of translations. The
staff are qualified book retailers, and shops have sofas for customers
to sit, unhurried and uninhibited, and read.

Books in Berlin Goethestraße 69, 31 31 233, www.booksinberlin.de.
Mon–Fri, open only in the afternoons. Comprehensive selection of
new and second-hand English language books. **Map p. 104, 1C**

Bücherbogen Knesebeckstraße 27, 886 83 695, www.buecherbogen.com.
International bookshop for art, architecture, photography and film.
The chain also has shops in the Neue Nationalgalerie (see p. 82) and
the Berggruen (see p. 113), though you might find cheaper prices
here. *U* to Uhlandstraße, *S* to Savignyplatz **Map p. 105, 1C**

Cantus 139 Kantstraße 139, 311 023 61, www.cantus139.de. Music
bookshop with a wide selection of sheet music in various genres.
Also stocks books about music and recordings from Bach to Brian
Jones. Offers a worldwide ordering and delivery service. *U* to
Uhlandstraße, *S* to Savignyplatz **Map p. 105, 1C**

Marga Schoeller Knesebeckstraße 33, 881 11 12. Closed Tue.
Independent bookshop with a good selection of fiction and non-
fiction in English, including German writers in translation. The staff
are very helpful and can answer enquiries, obtain books and make
recommendations. The shop recently celebrated its 75th
anniversary. *U* to Uhlandstraße **Map p. 105, 1C**

Guitar Shop Goethestraße 49 (electric) and 32 (acoustic), 31 25 607
(electric), 31 50 46 44 (acoustic). Welcome to guitar heaven. This
shop has been around for about 20 years and is an industry choice.
In electric there are 1,500 new and second-hand guitars and basses,

some vintage, some customised for the stars (including Eric Clapton's Fender), along with a wide selection of pedals and amplifiers. All instruments can be tried out in the sound-proofed room. *U* to Deutsche Oper **Map p. 104, 1C**

Hugendubel Tuentzienstraße 13, 01801 484 484, www.hugendubel.de. Hügendubel is one of Germany's biggest book-selling chains and this is their main Berlin store. They have a decent English section, though prices are usually higher than the UK/US jacket price. *U* to Kurfürstendamm **Map p. 105, 2C**

ACCESSORIES AND INTERIOR DESIGN

Art + Industry Bleibtreustraße 40, entry on Mommsenstraße, 883 49 46, open afternoons. Step into the Jazz era—collector's furniture and lamps ranging from Art Nouveau through Bauhaus and Art Deco to the 1970s and GDR. Also glass, ceramic, jewellery, watches, ornaments and electrical appliances. All the objects have been expertly restored and are sold at prices considerably lower than in the UK. There is a larger showroom at Wilmersdorferstraße 39. *U* to Uhlandstraße, *S* to Savignyplatz **Map p. 105, 1C**

Treykorn Savigny Platz 13, 31 80 23 54, www.treykorn.de. International designers of gold and silver jewellery exhibit their work in this gallery/shop. The unifying theme is modern but wearable designs, understated and geometric or weighty and decorative. Very interesting to look into, even if you're not planning on spending sizeable amounts of money. *U* to Uhlandstraße, *S* to Savignyplatz **Map p. 105, 1C**

GIFTS

Kaufhaus Des Westens (KaDeWe) Tauentzienstraße 21–24, 21 21 0. Berlin's oldest surviving department store, founded in 1907, 'aryanised' by the Nazis, and flaunted postwar as the symbol of western affluence and choice. When the wall fell, East Germans flocked here with their DM 100 'welcome money'. Six floors with everything a department store should have, including the legendary food hall on the sixth, with all manner of delicacies laid out at separate counters. *U* to Wittenbergplatz **Map p. 105, C3**

Lehmann's Colonialwaren Grolmannstraße 46, 883 39 42, open afternoons. Souvenirs from the age of discovery: compasses, model boats, globes, tennis racquets and travel bags. Also more unusual objects, such as a brass deep-sea diver's helmet or a six-foot-long dried shark. Perfect if you're looking for a little faded splendour for your home. *U* to Uhlandstraße, *S* to Savignyplatz **Map p. 105, 1C**

KREUZBERG

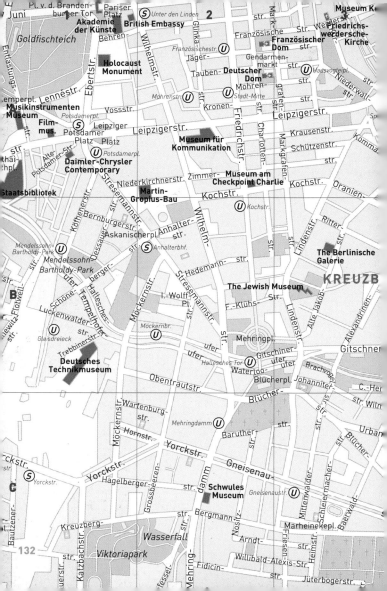

Stralauerstr.
Niederländische Botschaft
2
3
Rüdersdorfer
Singer-
Lichtenbe
Jannowitzbrücke

FRIEDRICHSHAIN

Fr.-Meh
Pl.
Holzmarkt-
Koppen-
Jannowitzbrücke
Märkisches Museum
Köllnischer Park
Spree
Kraut-
Lange-
Andreas-
der Pariser C
Wrie
Märkisches Museum

E.-Steinfurth-
str.
A
Heinrich-Heine-str.
Köpenicker-
Ostbahnhof
Ostbahnhof
Stralauerpl.

Schmidtstr.
Michaelstr.
Sebastianstr.
Annen-
Heinrich-Heine-Str.
Michaelkirchpl.
Mühlenstr.

Dresdener
Melchior-
damm
damm
str.
East Side Gallery
berstr.
H.-Heine-Pl.
Engel-
Bethanien-

Engelbecken
A.-Döblin-Pl.
Moritzpl.
Kunstlerhaus Bethanien
Wrangel-

Moritzpl.
Leuschner-
Waldemar-
Legiendamm
Mariannen-pl.
Muskauer-
Eisenbahn-
Pückler-
Zeughof-
Prinzenstr.
Oranienpl.
Naunyn-
NGBK
str.
B
Schlesisches To
Adalbert-
Kreuzberg Museum
Heinrichpl.
Mänteuffel-
Lausitzerpl.
Skalitzerstr.
str.
Kottbusser Tor
Skalitzerstr.
Wiener-
Görlitzerbhf.
str.
Wasser-torpl.
Görlitzer-
Zeughof-
Sorauerstr.
Oppelner-
lerpark
Zeglitz
Erkelenz
Kottbusser
Mariannen-
Spreewaldpl.
Görlitzerpar
banhafen
ufer
P.-Lincke-
Mänteuffel-
Reichenberger-
Plan-
Maybach-
Lausitzer-
Ohlauer-
Forster-
Liegnitzer-
Glogauer-
ufer Ratibor-
Dieffenbach-
Böckh-
Schinke-
Hobrecht-
Landwehrkanal
Grimmstr.
Schönleinstr.
str.
Bürkner-
Friedel-
Liberda-
Nansenstr.
C
Körtestr.
Fichtestr.
Graefe-
str.
Höhenstaufen-pl.
Sander-
Pflüger-
Bopp-str.
Lenau-
Reuter-
J) Südstern
Hasenheide
Urbanstr.
Weser-
Sonnenalle
Reuterpl.
Lohmühlenp
Hermannpl.
Pannier-
Hermannpl.

133

The Berlinische Galerie

OPEN *Main exhibition:* 12 pm–8 pm, Mon–Sat; 10 am–6 pm, Sun *Library:* 2 pm–8 pm, Mon–Fri *Eberhard-Roters-Saal:* 3 pm–6 pm, Mon–Fri (by appointment) *Study room:* 10 am–6 pm, Mon–Fri (by appointment)

CHARGES Main exhibition: Day ticket €5/€2. Free entry first Mon of the month. *Library:* Day ticket €1; year Ticket €8 *Eberhard-Roters-Saal:* Day ticket €3; Year ticket €40 *Study room:* Day ticket €10; month ticket €50; year ticket €200

ENTRANCE Alte Jakobstraße 124–128 U to Hallesches Tor or Kochstraße

TELEPHONE 78 90 26 00

WEB www.berlinischegalerie.de

SERVICES Cloakroom on ground floor near entrance

SHOP AND CAFÉ Bookshop at ground level, no ticket necessary. The inexpensive café has hours independent of gallery opening times and can be entered via the gallery or from the street.

HIGHLIGHTS

E.L. Kirchner's *Straßenszene*

Ludwig Meidner's *Jungste Tag*

George Grosz's *'Daum' Marries Her Pedantic Automaton 'George' in May 1920, John Heartfield is Very Glad of It*

Hannah Höch's *Dada Rundschau*

Ivan Puni's *Synthetischer Musiker*

El Lissitzky's *Prounen Raum*

Rudolf Schlichter *Sitzende Jenny*

Christian Schad's *Porträt des Schriftsteller Ludwig Bäumer*

Otto Dix's *Der Dichter Iwar von Lücken*

Max Bauer's *Reichskanzlei um 1935*

Rudolf Schlicter's *Blinde Macht*

Felix Nussbaum's *Selbstbildnis im Totenhemd*

Sergius Reugenberg's *Design for a Cinema in Berlin*

Fred Thieler's *Hommage à Tiepolo*

Eugen Schönebeck's *Der Gekreuzigte*

Eugen Schönebeck's *Ein moderne Maler*

Edward Kienholz's *Art Show*

Rainer Fetting's *Drummer and Guitarist*

Frank Thiel's *Wachregiment 'Friedrich Engels'*

THE COLLECTION

The Berlinische Galerie was founded in 1975 by Eberhard Röters to build a collection representing Berlin artists' contribution to 'the modern'—i.e., the period from 1900 to the present—and prevent these works from leaving Berlin.

At the time it was doubted whether the Berlinische Galerie was necessary. In 1968, the West German fine art collection had been returned to a situation approaching normality. International exhibitions shown in the van der Rohe building had given Berlin the reputation as a major city for contemporary art, and city planners were satisfied with the situation. The assumption was that whatever the Neue Nationalgalerie didn't pick up wasn't able to hold its own alongside international works, or was not art in the strict sense. To policy-makers whose ambitions were aimed at the west, a museum dedicated to Berlin alone committed the cardinal sin of provincialism.

Röters argued that below the surface of the apparent boom, the local scene had not, after thirty years, recovered from the damage done by National Socialism. Generations of artists had been murdered, exiled, or discouraged; oeuvres had been devalued and removed from the public eye. The result was a lack of faith in home-grown traditions, which in turn resulted in a dependency culture. Or, 'chalk dust from the last ruins still clings to the raw skin of their souls,' as Röters put it. When the wall fell in 1989, the BG's mandate doubled overnight as unification in art became necessary in parallel with political unification.

THE BUILDING

Since it was founded, the gallery had been aware that its home—in the Martin Gropius Bau—was provisional. For a while, the collection was put into storage throughout the city, while the major works went on tour around Europe. In 2002, a decision was made to occupy a former glass depot on Alte Jakob Straße. Aesthetically, the Glaswerk was not an obvious choice, but the building was structurally sound and required minimal conversion. The new premises opened in September 2004.

Situated between Mehring Platz and the Springer Verlag, and surrounded by council housing, all that draws the attention of passers-by is the glass foyer, with a raised back wall.

The new gallery is conceived of in terms not only of reflection but also usability. On the upper level is a room for researchers, a reading room and library. The Atelier Bunte Jakob is a children's art project used not only by visitors, but also local families keen to get the kids off their hands for a few hours.

EXPRESSIONISM

Straßenszene (1913–1915) by E.L. Kirchner With his move from Dresden to Berlin, Kirchner abandoned the nude and produced a large number of prints and drawings, full of nervous energy, capturing the frenetic motion of the city.

Jungste Tag (1916) by Ludwig Meidner Figures emerge from the shell-pocked landscape in a reference to Christian iconography of the Middle Ages, though now there is no representation of hell or paradise: a society without faith.

DADA

Dada Rundshau (1919) by Hannah Höch (See opposite page) The work is a photomontage of political events between 1914 and 1919, showing defeated Prussian generals Hindenburg, Ludendorff and Seeckt (bottom left), American president Woodrow Wilson (top),

Hannah Höch *Dada Rundshau* (1919)

Mathias Erzberger (centre) and the beer-bellied Reichspresident Ebert (who crushed the Spartacus uprising of 1919). The latter proclaimed that 'the spirit of the Weimar, the spirit of the great poets and philosophers, must once again fill our lives.' Höch comments drolly, 'Schatzkammer der Deutschen Gemütes entleert' ('Treasure chest of the German soul emptied out').

'Daum' Marries Her Pedantic Automaton 'George' in May 1920, John Heartfield is Very Glad of It (1920) by George Grosz Created on the occasion of Grosz's own marriage, the groom's chest whirrs with mechanical contraptions while hands feed random numbers into his empty head. Fellow Dadaist John Heartfield described the collage as 'a confession to a society that resembles a machine'.

EASTERN EUROPEAN AVANT-GARDE

Synthetischer Musiker (1921) by Ivan Puni A combination of the stylistic elements of Suprematism and realism, the painting seems to have been influenced by movies of Charlie Chaplin: not only does the musician wear white spats, bowler hat and moustache, but the effort of his playing causes his sleeves and coat tails to flap around.

Prounen Raum (1923, reconstruction 1965) by El Lissitzky The 'Proun' was a painting or relief in the form of a line, surface or sphere that could be combined in any number of ways in an interior. Lissitzky was concerned with social aesthetics, and intended that the Proun Room be adapted to a variety of domestic and industrial contexts.

NEW OBJECTIVITY

Sitzende Jenny (c. 1922–23) by Rudolf Schlichter A demonstration of a disillusioned perception of reality. The woman, with naked torso, modern hairstyle and dark make up, sits slackly on chair, staring at the viewer while unfastening her garter with her right hand.

Porträt des Schriftsteller Ludwig Bäumer (1927) by Christian Schad The Expressionist and revolutionary sympathies of a confident, well-groomed man are belied only by the orchids and the hall of mirrors behind.

Der Dichter Iwar von Lücken (1926) by Otto Dix The painting bears similarities to Karl Spitzweg's *Poet*, showing a bed-ridden poet crushing a flea. However while Spitzweg was placing the Romantic ideal of poetry in satirical contrast to the mundanity of the Biedermeier, Dix is sympathetic towards the Romantic melancholy of the grey-haired aristocrat.

ART UNDER NATIONAL SOCIALISM

Reichskanzlei um 1935 (1938–39, reprint 1995) by Max Bauer Though his work was printed as propaganda, Bauer was first and foremost as a technician of light. The polished, ox-blood marble interior was used postwar in U-bahn station Mohrenstraße.

Blinde Macht (1937) by Rudolf Schlichter A helmeted warrior stands at the edge of a chasm, a hellish landscape all around. He carries a set square and law books as war booty. Instead of a breastplate, grotesque creatures claw their way into his innards. In the same year this was painted, Schlicter's works were removed from public view and four of his graphic works shown in the *Entartete Kunst* exhibition. That this painting survived the war may have been due to its traditional, 'Old Master' style.

Selbstbildnis im Totenhemd (1942) by Felix Nussbaum. The artist's final painting before his murder follows Renaissance allegorical composition, with despair at the centre centre (holding the frayed rope), calm on the right, and accusation on the left (the only figure to look directly at the viewer). Nussbaum painted himself in the foreground, holding upright the branch of hope.

NEW BEGINNINGS

Design for a Cinema in Berlin (1946) by Sergius Reugenberg Reugenberg had been a draughtsman for Mies van der Rohe before the war; under Hans Scharoun he contributed to the revival of Berlin through an architecture that avoided lifeless grid forms.

FROM ABSTRACTION TO FIGURATION

Hommage à Tiepolo (1965) Fred Thieler The most important exponent of German Informel. This work has layers of printing ink applied at high speed, overlaid with torn strips of paper.

Der Gekreuzigte (1964) by Eugen Schönebeck The body reflects the tortured soul. **Schönebeck**, along with George Baselitz, wrote the *Pandemoniac Manifesto*, which owed much to Nietzsche and Artaut.

Ein moderne Maler (1966) Georg Baselitz The artist sits, legs spread and covered in paint, history carried in his rucksack.

THE 1970S AND BEYOND

The Art Show (1963-1977) by Edward Kienholz The figures in this installation were modelled on real personalities of the art scene. Keinholz and replaced their mouths with car fans, out of which come recorded art theoretical texts: hot air indeed.

Drummer and Guitarist (1979) by Rainer Fetting One of the '*Junge Wilden*' who grew up in the shadow of the wall, Fetting's works are loose colourful paintings expressing the search for authenticity in the Kreuzberg underground.

Wachregiment 'Friedrich Engels' (1990) by Frank Thiel Thiel's photographs are disconcertingly unrevealing, as the photographer explores the rituals of a regime in the process of disintegration. The portraits of the Soviet and American soldiers at Checkpoint Charlie are also by Thiel.

Daniel Libeskind's building for the Jewish Museum

The Jewish Museum

OPEN	The museum is open 10 am–8 pm (until 10 pm, Mon).
CHARGES	*Permanent exhibition:* €5/€2.50 *Temporary exhibition:* €4/€2 *Combined ticket:* €7/€3.50 *Combined family ticket:* €10. Ticket also provides entry to the Museum Blindwerkstatt Otto Weidt (see p. 145).
MAIN ENTRANCE	Lindenstraße 9–14
U-BAHN	U1 or U6 to Hallesches Tor
TELEPHONE	259 93 305, Tours: 030 259 93 305
WWW	jmberlin.de
SERVICES	The bookshop outside the main entrance has a wide range of books on Jewish themes. The Kosher restaurant, Liebermann's (€€; 25 93 97 71) has a moderately priced buffet between 12 pm and 4 pm, along with a snack bar between 10 am and 8 pm, and an afternoon tea buffet between 4 pm and 6 pm. Mon evenings 6 pm–10 pm is 'Oriental Buffet' with Klezmer accompaniment.

THE BUILDING

The Jewish Museum is one of the symbols of Berlin's post-reunification construction boom. In 1989, the Berlin Musem invited tenders for an extension to its existing premises, the Baroque Old Court House in Kreuzberg. The winning design was by Daniel Libeskind, whose reputation at that time was based on his teaching alone. The locals were sceptical: the design was considered unnecessarily esoteric and elitist. Critics were silenced when the building opened ten years and several building contractors later; the building has achieved genuine popularity both in Germany and internationally. Libeskind has since built the Felix Nussbaum building in Osnabrück, the Concert Hall in Bremen, the Victoria and Albert Museum extension, and most recently the Jewish museum in Copenhagen; his design for the World Trade Centre site awaits the go-ahead.

The floorplan was arrived at by drawing lines on a map between the former residences of well-known Jewish citizens of the city, resulting in a line bent nine times at acute angles, which some

THE JEWISH MUSEUM

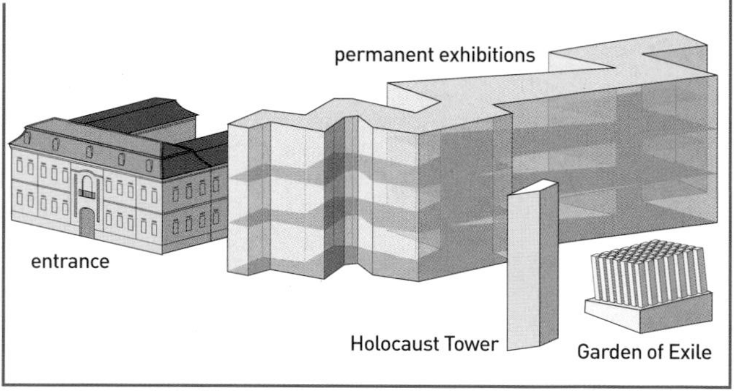

permanent exhibitions

entrance

Holocaust Tower

Garden of Exile

have compared to a shattered Star of David. A straight horizontal line cuts across the zig-zag, creating gaps in the structure which run through the three floors. The voids stage an absence within the 'body' of the building and represent the anihilation of the Jewish population of Berlin.

The windowless, and apparently impenetrable, zinc-faced walls give the building a forbidding appearance. Visitors enter via a staircase from the old museum, then pass through the basement to the 'axis of exile'. The disorientation created by the sloping floor is intended to evoke exile in a foreign culture; others see in it the deck of a ship at sea.

The path up the main corridor, the 'axis of continuity', is intersected by the 'axis of the Holocaust'. This leads up to the Holocaust tower, a tall concrete construction like an air-raid bunker. A small slit in the top corner lets in sound and light; a ladder too high to reach confounds hopes of escape. In summer the space is cold, in winter freezing.

The 'axis of continuity' leads to the main stairs, the most spectacular feature of the design, with its criss-cross of girders and patterns of light. The stairway gives onto the ground floor gallery; walking through brings you to the largest of the voids, the 'memory void'. Menashe Kadishman has created an installation

THE JEWISH MUSEUM

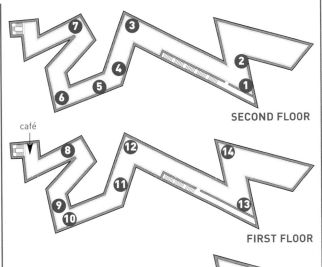

SECOND FLOOR

café

FIRST FLOOR

memory void

gallery

UNDERGROUND LEVEL

1 Beginnings
2 The Medieval World of Ashkenaz
3 Glikl bas Juda Leib
4 Rural and Court Jews
5 Moses Mendelssohn and the Enlightenment
6 Tradition and Change
7 The Heart of the Family
8 Same Responsibilities - Same Rights?
9 The Emergence of Modern Judaism

10 Modernism and Urban Life
11 East and West
12 German Jews, Jewish Germans
13 Persecution - Resistance - Extermination
14 The Present

there entitled *Shalachet* ('Fallen Leaves'), a floor covered with circular railway parts, each with a face cut out of it, recalling the transport of Jews to the camps by rail.

The first and second floors hold the permanent exhibition. The third floor is administration. Temporary exhibitions are held in the Old Museum. In the basement of the new building is the Rafael Roth Learning Centre, an electronic archive. Built into the walls of the axes are display cabinets containing objects donated to the museum by victims of National Socialism, such as the certificates of racial origin that 'suspected Jews' were obliged to present.

THE PERMANENT EXHIBITION

The permanent exhibition begins on the **second floor**. It is arranged chronologically and thematically, beginning with early Judaica in parallel with exhibits showing the roots of Christian antisemitism in medieval times. A focus on the the medieval town of Wurms shows the organisation of the Jewish quarter and the symbiosis between Jewish and Christian populations.

The early modern period is traced through individual biographies, like that of Glikl bas Juda Leib, the daughter of a wealthy Hamburg trading family and the earliest known female memoirist. This was the era of the 'Court Jew', who in return for contributions to the country received special favours from the ruling house; Joseph Süss Oppenheimer, financial adviser to Alexander of Würtemmburg, was a famous example. When his patron died, his enemies had him executed, and his story has provided the blueprint for the downfall of the 'demonic' Jew ever since.

The section on the 18th C describes the gradual modernisation of Judaism in response to European currents of thought, initiated above all by Moses Mendelssohn, who came to Berlin in 1743 as a Talmud scholar. His book, *Phaedon, or On the Immortality of the Soul*, earned hime the title of 'the German Socrates'.

The exhibition continues on the first floor with the 19th Century and the founding of the German empire in 1871, under which Jews were recognised as individual citizens.

The section on the turn of the 20th Century concentrates on the Jewish contribution to the commercial and cultural life of Berlin, at that time home to a quarter of all German Jews. Hermann Wallich, for example, was a founder of Deutsche Bank; Otto Brahms was the founder of 'naturalistic theatre'. Other luminaries include musicians Kurt Weill and Arnold Schönberg, philosophers Walter Benjamin, Georg Simmel and Siegfried Krakauer, and, of course, Albert Einstein.

The emancipation brought by the Weimar Republic was short-lived, and marred by the census meant to catch Jewish conscription 'shirkers'. Walter Rathenau, the foreign minister, was murdered by a right wing organisation in 1922; the beginning of the end came with the 'Law of the Restoration of the Civil Service' of 1933, when 3,000 Jewish civil servants were removed from their posts.

The exhibition ends with the war trials and the so-called process of '*Vergangenheitsbewaltigung*', or coming to terms with the past. The reactions of the new, radicalised generation of Jews are seen in a television reportage of the sabotaging of a play by Rainer Werner Fassbinder in the 1970s; protesters accused it of replaying antisemitic stereotypes. However, the Jewish philospher Theodor Adorno provides the parting word in saying that any attempt to silence supposed anti-Semitism implies it contains some truth.

MUSEUM BLINDWERKSTATT OTTO WEIDT

Rosenthaler Straße 39, 28 59 94 07, www.blindes-vertrauen.de. 12 pm–8 pm, Mon–Fri; 11 am–8 pm, Sat–Sun.

The Museum Blindwerkstatt Otto Weidt houses 'Blind Faith: Hidden at the Hackescher Markt', based on accounts of life under the threat of deportation. The building is on the premises of a former broom factory staffed entirely by blind and deaf Jews during the 1930s. The exhibit tracks the efforts of employer Otto Weidt to prevent his employees from being taken. The museum is aimed particularly at younger visitors.

in the area

Deutsches Technikmuseum Trebbiner Straße 9, 90 25 41 11, www.dtmb.de. 9 am–5.30 pm, Tue–Fri; 10 am–6 pm, Sat–Sun. In the former goods station of the Anhalter Bahnhof, a shrine to Deutsche know-how. Unmissable as you ride past on the U-bahn because of the airlift-era Allied DC3 attached to the roof. Pride of place goes to the locomotives and rolling stock from 1835 to the present. Also has old-time aeroplanes, steam engines, computers, radios, printing presses and household technology, with plenty of chances for interactivity. *U* to Möckernbrücke **Map p. 132, 1B**

Kreuzberg Museum Adalbertstraße 95a, 50 58 52 33, www.kreuzberg museum.de. 12 pm–6 pm, Wed–Sun. Museum on the history of district SO36: getting there involves walking through Kottbusser Tor, Berlin at its most down-at-heel. Three floors show the history of the printworks formerly on the site, town planning and the counter-culture movement during the 1960 and 1970s, and an exhibition is planned on the history of migration in the district. **Map p. 133, 2B**

Kunstlerhaus Bethanien Mariannenplatz 2, 616 90 30, www.bethanien.de. 2 pm–7 pm, Wed–Sun. This former hospital was used as a huge squat until 1973, when it came up for demolition. It was saved by the organisation that still occupies the building. International artists in residence occupy the 25 studios and hold exhibitions in the three exhibition rooms open to the public. *U* to Kottbusser Tor **Map p. 133, 2B**

Martin-Gropius-Bau Niederkirchenerstraße 7, 254 86 05, 10 am–9 pm, closed Tuesdays. Neo-Renaissance building from 1881 by Martin Gropius, pupil at Schinkel's Bauakademie. Its imitation palazzo, polychrome façade contrasts with the Neo-Classical grandeur of the Museumsinsel complex. The gallery holds two or three travelling exhibitions at any one time, and also has a well-stocked bookshop and a café. Next door is the Topography of Terrors, a temporary photographic exhibition about National Socialism located in the cellers of the former HQ of the Schutzstaffel (SS) and the Geheim Staatspolizeiamt (Gestapo). Construction work on a permanent museum on the site has run over budget and been shelved. *U* to Kochstraße **Map p. 132, 2A**

Museum am Checkpoint Charlie Friedrichstraße 44, 253 725 11, www.mauer-museum.com. 9 am–10 pm. Frank Thiel's photographs of young border guards stare down the length of the Friedrichstraße, next to the sign 'You are leaving the American Sector'. The Haus am Checkpoint Charlie was the last building before the border of the eastern

Zone, and western anti-wall campaigners used it as an observation point for comings and goings. The building now houses a museum with fascinating documentation, film, photographs and artifacts about the Mauer and the Mauerspringer ('wall jumpers'). Recently a section of the wall has been rebuilt at Checkpoint Charlie, along with wooden crosses commemorating people killed trying to cross to the West. Critics have called the monument unimaginative and accused the museum of commercialising history. *U* to Kochstraße **Map p. 132, 2A**

Neue Gesellshaft fur Bildende Kunst (NGBK) Oranienstraße 25, 615 30 31, www.ngbk.de. 12 pm–6.30 pm. A contemporary non-commercial gallery affiliated to the West Berlin artists' collective; all exhibitions are produced and created by members. One of its working groups is the Alexanderplatz U2 group, responsible for the installations on the U-bahn platform. The emphsis is on artwork of a social-critical and conceptual nature; this is the place to see what's cutting it on the off-scene. *U* to Kottbusser Tor **Map p. 133, 2B**

Schwules Museum Mehringdamm 61, 693 11 72, www.schwules museum.de. 2 pm–6 pm, Mon, Wed, Fri, Sun; 2 pm–7 pm, Sat. Museum and documentation centre for all facets of homosexual life, with a focus on biography. Holds temporary exhibitions relating to homosexual culture. *U* to Hallesches Tor **Map p. 132, C2**

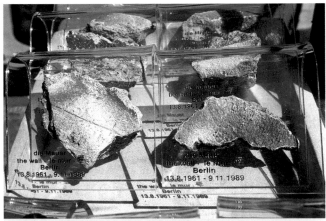

Pieces of the wall for sale at Checkpoint Charlie

commercial galleries

Galerie Sievi Gneisenaustraße 112, 693 29 97, www.artfacts.net.de/sievi.
4 pm–7 pm, Tue–Thu; 3 pm–7 pm, Sat; 11 am–3 pm. Figurative abstraction, Informel. *U* to Mehringdamm or Gneisenaustraße. **Map p. 132, 2C**

Galerie Tammen & Busch Chamissoplatz 6, 694 012 45, www.tammen-busch.de. 11 am–2 pm, Sat; 3 pm–6 pm, Sun. Movements in younger Berlin painting. *U* to Platz der Luftbrücke **Map p. 132, 2C**

eat

RESTAURANTS

€ **Café Adler** Friedrich Straße 206, 251 8965. Adler's location directly opposite Checkpoint Charlie means there is a mark-up, but it's a good place to go for *Mohnkuchen* (cake made from poppy seeds) or *apfelstrudel mit vanillesoße*. On the site of a former chemist's, it retains its 1920s feel, with mirrors and gold fittings. A cheaper alternative is to go a block down the road to the Lekkerbeck (211-212)—a no nonsense canteen where you can get a hot meal for under €5. **Map p. 132, 2A**

Blue Nile Tempelhofer Ufer 6, 25 29 46 55, www.bluenileethio.de. An Ethiopian bar and restaurant specialising in the Wot, a spicy stew served with Injera, the traditional bread. Coffee is not only a major Ethiopian export but also prized in the country itself, and on Sat and Sun from 8 pm the Blue Nile has a coffee ceremony: the beans are roasted, brewed and served to guests with popcorn. You can eat for under €10. *U* to Hallesches Tor **Map p. 132, 2B**

The Ice Cream Parlour Falckensteinstraße 7. Papaya, peach, mango, melon, Black Forest cherry, kiwi...spaghetti? Yes, spaghetti ice cream is a firm Berlin favourite: squiggles of vanilla ice cream with strawberry sauce. This backstreet ice cream parlour is a kids' paradise and popular with grown-ups too. An oasis of colour, with palm trees and tropical flower arrangements, it's a feast for the eyes, too. *U* to Schlesiches Tor **Map p. 157, 3C**

Knofi Bergmannstraße 98, 694 56 44. 9 am–10 pm, Mon–Fri; 8 am–5 pm, Sat. This wonderfully stocked deli has foods from all over Europe, and the goodies can can be sampled at the small café. Four menus, all for €4 or less, offer a selection of homemade vegetarian pastes and spreads with bread. Also try the wines, coffee, pasta, oils, nuts, jams and crystallised fruit. *U* to Gneisenaustraße **Map p. 132, 2C**

Turkiyem Imbiss Schlesiches Straße 1, 611 8492. This is the largest establishment on Kreuzberg's döner corner, and open 24 hours every day. The staff are always cheerful. To help you out: '*gleich essen*' means you want to eat the döner right away, '*einpacken*' means wrapped for later. A '*Pommes Rot/Weiss*' is chips with ketchup and mayo. (It's a great place to begin or end a tour of Kreuzberg's bars.) *U* to Schlesiches Tor **Map p. 157, 3C**

€€ Amrit Oranienstraße 202/203, 612 55 50, www.amrit.de. Indian restaurant with branches on the Oranienburger Straße and Nollendorfplatz. What the dishes lack in spiciness (the German palate is famously bland, so for 'hot' on the menu read 'mild'), they make up for in flavour. The lamb is juicy and the vegetarian dishes delicate and fresh. For something a bit special try the tandoori grill brought sizzling to the table. The portions are generous and it's well worth the €15 or so a head you'll spend, including popadams and drinks. *U* to Görlitzer Bahnhof **Map p. 133, 2B**

Il Casolare Grimmstraße 30, corner of Planufer, 69 50 66 10, www.ilcasolaredikreuzberginrete.it. A genuine Italian pizzeria in Berlin's greenest district; the views of the canal give the area an Amsterdam-like feel. Come here after a walk through the Turkish Market on the Maybach Ufer. Il Casolare is always busy, so you might want to book. *U* to Kottbusser Tor **Map p. 133, 1C**

Iskele Planufer 82, 69 50 72 65. From 11 am, Apr–Sept; from 4 pm, Oct–Mar. Turkish fish restaurant in a barge afloat the Landwehr Canal (the fish are caught elsewhere, we've been assured). Iskele is open-air in the summer and has live music at the weekend. A good place to watch Kreuzbergers on their home turf and get a taste of Berlin's most diverse district. *U* to Kottbusser Tor **Map p. 133, 1C**

Markthalle Pücklerstraße 34, 617 55 02. 9 am–2 pm, Sun–Thur; 9 am–6 am, Fri–Sat. Extremely popular bar and restaurant, not to be confused with the other Markthalle on Bergmannstrasse. Wood-panelled interior and excellent German cuisine, featuring seasonal specialities, open until midnight every night. It featured in the recent Berlin film 'Herr Lehmann.' Open till the early hours on weekends. Recommended. **Map p. 133, 3B**

Ossena Oranienstraße 39, 615 26 22. Italian restaurant especially recommended for its pizzas and family-sized portions of pasta. Friendly waiters and comfortable sitting area upstairs. This is the original Ossena; it has been so successful that two more have opened in Mitte, at Oranienburgerstraße 39 and Rosenthaler Straße 42. **U** to Moritzplatz **Map p. 133, 1B**

€€€Restaurant H.H. Müller Im Umspannwerk, Paul Lincke Ufer 20, 61 07 67 60. 12 pm–1 am, Sun–Fri; 6 pm–1 am, Sat. A restaurant in a converted generating station built in the 1920s by architect H.H. Müller. The interior design is spectacular; tables for two on the mezzanine offer a highly unusual eating experience, and in warm weather there are seats outside. The cuisine is top notch and describes itself as Swiss international. The position of the restaurant allows for a promenade along the Ufer, one of the most pleasant walks in the city. **U** to Schönleinstraße **Map p. 133, 3C**

 # BARS

Ankerklause Kottburser Damm 104/Maybach Ufer. 693 5649, www.ankerklause.de. 10 am–5am, Tue–Sun; 4pm–5am, Mon. Kitchen until 4 pm. The 'Anchor Bar' is a firm Berlin favourite and always has a great atmosphere. Thur is disco night. Recommended. **U** to Schönleinstraße. **Map p. 133, 2C**

Bar Atlantic Bergmannstraße 100, 691 92 92. 9 am–2 am. Breakfast until 5 pm, lunch until midnight, happy hour every day between 8 pm and 9 pm. With a decent menu at cheapish prices, this bar is always busy, but big enough that you can find a table. A good place to sit outside on warm evenings and watch the comings and goings along the Bergmannstraße. **U** to Gneisenaustraße **Map p. 132, 2C**

Bar der Visionär Am Flut Grab 2, off Schlesiche Straße. Late opening hours. Open air bar on the water's edge, with house DJs every night of the week, beginning in the afternoon. Get a caipirinha (€6.50) after a swim in the Badeshiff, the open air swimming pool afloat the Spree (Eichenstraße 4, behind the arena, www.badeschiff.de). **Map p. 157, 3C**

Bateaux Ivre Oranienstraße 19, 61 40 36 59. 9 am–3 am. Famous and well-placed Kreuzberg hang-out. Serves breakfast and lunch until 4 pm. They usually have the day's *Guardian* or *Herald Tribune*. Later the place gets busy; you can order tapas, but the emphasis is on drinking. There's always a crowd of locals in here, and though the drinks aren't the cheapest, the atmosphere never fails to work. *U* to Görlitzer Bahnhof **Map p. 133, 2B**

Franken Oranienstraße 19a, 614 10 81. 10 pm–5 am. A rocker's bar, with pinball and a wild boar's head hanging over the bar. Gritty, sociable, with dogs wandering around. Cocktails for €4.50. **Map p. 133, 2B**

Konrad Tönz Falckensteinstraße 30, 612 32 52, www.konradtoenzbar.de. 8.15 pm onwards, closed Mon. This bar (the name is taken from a 1970s Swiss TV crime series) is a piece of interior design genius: flawless retro, with lots of Op Art wall paper, lava lamps and shellac-topped coffee tables. DJs play soul, psychedelic and garage on the ultra lo-fi turntable. *U* to Schlesiches Tor **Map p. 157, 3C**

Möbel Olfe Dresdener Straße, walkway to Kottbusser Tor, 23 27 46 90. From 6 pm onwards, closed Mon. Drink a Rathaus Pils (one of the best bottled beers on the market) and watch local Turkish mums push prams. This bar has a glass front onto Kreuzberg's most urban corner; its bare concrete walls add to its underground carpark feel. Olfe is popular with a diverse and humorous mixed/gay crowd who party at the weekend. Not to be missed. *U* to Kottbusser Tor **Map p. 133, 1B**

The Old Emerald Isle Erkelenzendamm 49, 615 69 17, www.old-emerald-isle.de. From 12 pm onwards, kitchen until 12 am. Probably Berlin's best Irish pub, tucked away in a leafy corner of Kreuzberg. Has a solid menu ranging from sandwiches through burgers to Irish stew. Always busy with a relaxed and party-minded international crowd; live football also helps shift the Guinness. *U* to Kottbusser Tor **Map p. 133, 1B**

San Remo Falckensteinstraße 49, 61 28 679. Open-end hours. Well-placed on the cusp of Friedrichshain and Kreuzberg, this is a popular early evening kick-off for a tour of the bars. Casual and unpretentious, with a wooden table and a plain brick interior, and seating on the pavement in the summer. DJs at the weekend. *U* to Schlesiches Tor **Map p. 157, 3C**

Wiener Blut Wiener Straße 14, 618 90 23. Open from 6 pm onwards, Mon–Sat (or from 3 pm in football season); from 4 pm, Sun. The archetypal red bar and the best that the Wienerstraße strip has to offer. Lots of comfy seating, with table football and a TV for live sport. Music is ska with some techno thrown in. *U* to Görlitzer Bahnhof **Map p. 133, 2B**

Würgeengel Dresdener Straße 122, 615 55 60, www.wuergeengel.de. From 7 pm onwards. Red velvet seating, a Jugendstil ceiling and hanging lamps, staff in black and white: this cocktail bar of repute, named after Buñuel's film 'Exterminating Angel', has a down-beat classicism popular with local artist types. Also does tapas and Italian food. *U* to Kottbusser Tor **Map p. 133, 1B**

shop

CLOTHING

uko fashion Oranienstraße 201, 693 81 16, www.uko-fashion.de. 11 am–8 pm, Mon–Fri; 11 am–4 pm, Sat. Street, sexy and elegant designer wear for women, including Free Soul and Pussy Deluxe (underwear): second season and model sets mean knock-down prices. Also good quality, carefully chosen second-hand clothing and accessories. For the chic but cost-conscious Kreuzbergerin. *U* to Görlitzer Bahnhof **Map p. 133, 2B**

Ritchie Oranienstraße 174, 615 91 65, www.ritchie.de. Women's wear by young Berlin designers, as well as big names like Fornarina and Lolita. Bright and up-front: a good bet if you're looking for something to wear when you hit the clubs. *U* to Görlitzer Bahnhof **Map p. 133, 2B**

Faster Pussycat Mehringdamm 57, 69 50 66 00. 11 am–8 pm, Mon–Fri; 11 am–5 pm, Sat. All-new gear for women, funky and eyecatching with a distinct retro flavour. Also has shoes, bags, jewellery and a good range of wigs, if you happen to need one. A furniture section at the back sells second-hand 1960s and 1970s furniture and fittings gleaned from the flea markets. *U* to Mehringdamm **Map p. 132, 2C**

Killerbeast Wrangelstraße 48, 99 26 03 19, www.killerbeast.de. 12 pm–7.30 pm, Tue–Fri; 10 am–2 pm, Sat. In the middle of one of Kreuzberg's poorest districts, a brilliant fashion concept has taken root: customers bring old articles of clothing (or even tablecloths, curtains or bed linens) and have them pepped up into highly original, tailormade clothing. Shirts cost around €39 and jeans €89; they can be turned around in four days. **U** to Schlesiches Tor **Map p. 133, 3B**

Shuhtanten Paul Lincke Ufer 44, 61 62 97 56, www.schuhtanten.de. 11 am–7 pm, Mon–Fri; 11 am–4 pm, Sat. 'Shoes you want to bite' is how this small but exquisite shop describes its wares. Women's shoes from Italy, Spain, Denmark and Russia, clogs to high heels, flip flops to ballet pumps...all the shoes are overstock and thus are very inexpensive. A friendly and sympathetic staff create an atmosphere conducive to making those difficult decisions. **U** to Schönleinstraße **Map p. 133, 2B**

Lucid 21 Mariannenstraße 50, 0173 783 1951, www.lucid21.net. 12 am–7 pm, Tue–Fri; 10 am–4 pm, Sat. Small shop selling clothing and accessories designed by Luis Gunsch for the Berlin label. Particularly well-known for minimal and close-cut numbers printed with cutsey animal pictures. Big in Japan. **U** to Görlitzer Bahnhof **Map p. 133, 2B**

BOOKS AND MUSIC

Another Country Riemannstraße 17, www.anothercountry.de. 11 am–8 pm, Mon–Fri; 11 am–4 pm, Sat. An institution for literary expats, Another Country operates as a lending library for English language books. You put down a deposit, which you get back minus a small user's fee when you return the book. Regulars stop by for a chat with Alan Raphaeline, the unflappable owner. Literary evenings also happen at regular intervals. **U** to Gneisenaustraße **Map p. 132, 2C**

Grober Unfug Zossener Straße 33, 69 40 14 90, www.groberunfug.de. 11 am–7 pm, Mon–Fri; 11 am–4 pm, Sat. *'Grober Unfug'* means 'crude nonsense'. The international section on the 1st floor has an exhaustive selection of comics, graphic novels, cartoons, posters and movie props. **U** to Gneisenaustraße **Map p. 132, 3C**

Scratch Records Zossener Straße 31, 6981 7591. 11 am–7 pm, Mon–Wed; 11 am–8 pm, Thur–Fri; 10 am–4 pm, Sat. Small independent record shop with a select stock, including hip hop, soul, alternative, folk and world music, in vinyl and CD. Lots of bargain prices. You can listen before you buy and the owner is well informed and helpful. **U** to Gneisenaustraße **Map p. 132, 3C**

Space Hall Zossener Straße 33, 694 76 64, www.spacehall.de. 10 am–7 pm, Mon–Wed; 11 am–8 pm, Thur–Fri; 10 am–4 pm, Sat.

Kreuzeberg's biggest record shop, with both new and used stock. Specialises in electronica: no genre is too rare, no artist too underground. Plenty of decks to listen to the records. Visit the gallery at Bergmannstraße 5–7: the former supermarket is now a shop and lounge with a beer garden in the courtyard, open until 8 pm. *U* to Gneisenaustraße **Map p. 132, 3C**

ACCESSORIES AND INTERIOR DESIGN

BagAge Bergmannstraße 13, 693 89 16, www.bag-age.de. 11 am–8 pm, Mon–Fri; 10 am–4 pm, Sat. Bike and messenger bags, backpacks, bowling bags, airliner bags...look out for the Kultbag label, which soups up old GDR postal bags or army bags with materials such as felt, rubber tyres or 1970s air mattresses. Also popular are the laptop bags, featuring labels including Manhattan Portage, TaTü, Leonca, Lumabag and Tita Berlin. **Map p. 132, 2C**

Bella Casa Bergmannstraße 101, 694 07 84, www.bella-casa-berlin.de. 11 am–8 pm, Mon–Fri; 10 am–5 pm, Sat. Specialising in products from India, North Africa and the Near and Middle East. The focus is on interior design, with cushions, lamps, wall hangings and tiles. The shop also has a wide range of materials; buy damask and moirée by the metre. All the stock is acquired by the owner on his travels around the world. **Map p. 132, 2C**

GIFTS

Hanf Haus Oranienstraße 192, 614 81 02. 11 am–7 pm, Mon–Fri; 11 am–4 pm, Sat. Not a head shop! The versatile plant is represented here in all its legal uses: nibble on hemp seeds, pour hemp oil on your salad, rub hemp lotion into your skin, wear a hempen shirt. **Map p. 133, 2B**

MARKETS

Markthalle Bergmann Straße east end. Indoor market with a full range of stalls, from socks to sandwiches. It's the one-stop-shop for the everyday needs of the locals. At the back, the Gasthaus Herz offers Wienerschnitzel for €6 and barbequed steaks for €8. Laid-back Kreuzbergers drink Schultheiss in the beer garden while their kids splash about in the fountain. *U* to Gneisenaustraße **Map p. 132, 2C**

Turkish Market on the Maybachufer 781 58 44. 12 pm–6.30, Tue and Fri. Famous food market, better and cheaper than what's offered in the supermarket. Also flat bread, olives, sheep's cheese, baklava...an affectionate nickname for Kreuzberg is 'little Istanbul'. *U* to Schönleinstraße **Map p. 132, 3C**

FRIEDRICHSHAIN AND PRENZLAUERBERG

FRIEDRICHSHAIN, with its docks, was historically an industrial district; Sartre mentions its long, broad and windy streets as an area 'near warehouses, tram depots, slaughterhouses and gas works.' Now Universal Music and MTV occupy Sartre's warehouses, but Friedrichshain remains a little downmarket. It is favoured by students, and areas around Ostkreuz station retain a genuine 'east' feel.

PRENZLAUERBERG was a residential, working-class district until World War II, but under the GDR it became a centre for artists (the wall separating Prenzlauerberg from Wedding in the west ran along Bernauer Straße up to the bridge at Bornholmer Straße). The district was a brief paradise for the alternative squatting lifestyle in the 1990s, but by the end of the decade developers had won the day and gentrification is now complete in Prenzlauerberg. Now the vast majority of the population are western German 'Wahl Berliners' ('Berliners by choice'), whose family-mindedness have caused the birth rate in the district to soar (earning Prenzlauerberg the nickname 'Babyberg'). This concentration of youth and money means that Prenzlauerberg's shops and cafés are renowned for their trendiness.

Getting from Prenzlauerberg to Friedrichshain is easy: take Tram 20 from Eberswalder Straße/Warschauer Straße.

Gedenkstätte Normannenstrasse

THE FORMER MINISTRY FOR STATE SECURITY (STASI)

OPEN	The museum is open 11 am–6 pm, Mon–Fri; 2 pm–6 pm, Sat, Sun.
CHARGES	€3.50/€2.50; groups of over ten, €2.50/€2 per person
MAIN ENTRANCE	Ruschestraße 103
TELEPHONE	553 68 54
WEB	www.stasi-museum.de
U-BAHN	Magadalenenstraße (U5)
SERVICES	The general's café is on the 1st floor. There is a bookshop on the ground floor with an extensive selection of material on the GDR and Stasi.
TOURS	Tours in English can be arranged in advance for groups of ten or more. If you are on your own, either join one of the regular group tours or pay €25 for a private tour. Alternatively, you can purchase a guide book to the museum at the front desk.

This ten-hectare complex in the eastern district of Lichtenberg was the former residency of the Ministry for State Security (the MfS, or Stasi). Since 1990, the site has been a museum and archive.

THE STASI

The German Democratic Republic was a one-party state ruled by the SED (German Socialist Unity Party). Its intelligence department, the Stasi, referred to itself as the 'the sword and shield of the party,' pursuing and persecuting 'class enemies from outside and within'. They did this until the collapse of the GDR in 1989. When established in 1950, the Stasi had around one thousand members; in 1989 it had 91,000 official members, of whom 20,000 worked at the Normannenstraße site. A further

A recording device in Mielke's office at Stasi HQ

174,000 people were counted as 'unofficial members', including 15,000 in West Germany. Of a total population of 6.4 million, this meant that around one person in sixty had links to the Stasi. The Stasi imprisoned around 250,000 people in a total of fifteen centres, including Berlin Hohenschönhausen and Berlin Rummelsberg.

When the Berlin wall fell, on Nov 9, 1989, people soon occupied the Normannen-straße site and began sifting through the documents (though it is thought that they were directed away from highly sensitive material).

Administrative responsibility for the museum and archive was handed over to 'Anti-Stalinist Action Normannenstraße' (ASTAK), a citizens' and civil rights coalition. In 1999 a media centre was installed for viewing videos, documents and other archive material.

THE MUSEUM

Haus 1 now houses the museum. The **ground floor** has documentary material on the Stasi, along with surveillance equipment and ceremonial paraphernalia. The **first floor** has been preserved as it was found in 1989: the marbled foyer, conference room, lounge and cafeteria, as well as the minister's offices. The wall-to-wall wood panelling and red carpet are typical of the flimsy modernist chic favoured by the GDR political elite during the 1960s and 1970s. Of special interest is the office of Erich Mielke, the Stasi commander-in-chief, which has been perfectly preserved.

The second floor has a two-part exhibition, starting with photos, texts and memorabilia about resistance during the regime—from Social Democratic movements, the Church, writers and artists, and youth movements. The second part of the exhibition documents the major events during 'the peaceful revolution' of 1989.

The former SED elite met ignominious ends. Erich Honecker, the president from 1971, was expelled from the party in 1989 and fled to Moscow. He was extradited by the Russians and spent two years in prison in Berlin. After his release, on health grounds, he went to Santiago in Chile, where he died in 1995. Mielke was imprisoned in Berlin Moabit between 1992 and 95, charged with the murder of two policemen in 1931. He was released on health grounds and died in Berlin in 2000. Former Stasi members today are shunned and receive reduced 'punishment' pensions. Public figures are routinely embarassed by their Stasi files, now available to the public.

KulturBrauerei

OPEN	Always open
CHARGES	Free
MAIN ENTRANCE	Knaackstraße 97
TELEPHONE	44 31 51 52
WEB	www.kulturbrauerei-berlin.de
U-BAHN	Eberswalder Straße (U2)

THE BUILDING

The KulturBrauerei is an enormous cultural centre at the gate of Prenzlauerberg, founded in 1991 on the site of the restored Shultheiss Brewery Complex. The original buildings were built by Franz Schwechten (architect of the Kaiser Wilhelm

Gedächtniskirche and Anhalter Güter Bahnhof) in 1890. It marked the transition to mechanised brewing techniques and catapulted Schultheiss to the forefront of the industry (where it remains). The functional neo-Romanesque design, using brick and iron, was in tune with the industrial sprit of the *Gründerzeit*.

SAMMLUNG INDUSTRIELLE GESTALTUNG
(INDUSTRIAL DESIGN COLLECTION)

OPEN	1 pm–8 pm, Wed–Sun (subject to change)
CHARGES	€2/€1
MAIN ENTRANCE	Knaackstraße 97
TELEPHONE	44 31 78 68

The Industrial Design Collection moved into the north wing of the Schultheiss brewery complex in 1993. The museum records the development of product design in the GDR from 1945 to 1990, and includes glassware, ceramics, precision mechanics (watches, typewriters, measuring instruments), optical and phonographic instruments (cameras, radios, televisions), toys, lighting and furniture. Advertising, propaganda posters and print media can also be found in the collection. Exhibitions change regularly.

   The collection provides a record of people's relations to the GDR system, one that veered between optimism and dismay. Postwar Germany provided a seedbed for idealists eager to reinstate democracy, peace and humanism. This extended to product design; as Mart Stam wrote, 'we want a final form, an industrial form'. This would come about when manufacturers 'refer to human needs and seek ways to fulfil these'. The fruit of this idealism was the groundbreaking architecture and design realised in the short period between 1945 and 1950.

Utopian ideals disappeared during the Cold War, as art and design were conscripted in the fight against the 'class enemy'. A political leadership in thrall to the Soviet Union denounced avant-garde movements in architecture, design and typography. This reactionary current affected architecture especially, where the required style was a mix of monumental 19th-C classicism and Socialist Realism (see the Karl-Marx-Allee, Frankfurter Allee and the surrounding apartment blocks for examples of this heavy-handed style).

A short-lived period of economic growth in the 1960s saw a design boom, although the Hoenecker era dealt a further blow to those with hopes for a democratic society. Nevertheless, an unmistakable design identity developed in the GDR. In a market without competition, product designers didn't need to generate demand through stylistic novelty, but could concentrate on more 'rational' values: form versus function, and simplicity and usability.

Since it was forbidden to awake people's desire for objects they would have to wait years for (cars above all), products such as cough mixture, washing powder, mosquito spray or black and white film became highly desirable. Since products were not required to differentiate themselves from competing brands, packaging favoured a refined, toned-down aesthetic.

Nowadays, principles such as 'longevity', 'anti-style' and 'simplicity' are buzz words for contemporary designers. What was, back then, a way of getting round material shortages has become a back-to-basics design philosophy. The trend for Ost Produkte can be seen in shops such as Schönhauser or re-store in Mitte (see pp. 65 and 64), Hit-In.TV or Thatchers in Prenzlauerberg (see p. 175), and Berlinomat in Friedrichshain (see p. 175). For original GDR objects, try the Intershop2000 in Friedrichshain (see p. 175), or the flea markets on Arkonaplatz or Boxhagener Platz.

MANUFACTUM OUTLET AT THE SAMMLUNG INDUSTRIELLE GESTALTUNG

44 31 78 68, www.manufactum.de. 1 pm–8 pm, Wed–Sun

Manufactum is a retailer for international product designers. The products range from kitchen equipment through interior design to tools, and are chosen for their high production standards, durability and repairability. Design favours classical materials and form after function.

KESSELHAUS

44 31 50; office open 10 am–6 pm, Mon–Fri

The large underground vat chamber is now used for concerts, and has a good reputation as a venue for Eastern European and Francophone music.

KINO IN DER KULTURBRAUEREI

44 35 44 22

Multi-screen cinema with high-tech projectors and sound reproduction, also lots of leg room and a steep incline allowing excellent viewing. Tends to feature off-Hollywood productions, usually dubbed into German.

LITERATURWERKSTATT

48 52 45 0, www.literaturwerkstatt.org

A literature forum with a varied international programme, announced monthly (check the website). English language authors appear regularly.

BEER GARDEN

72 62 79 30; From 4 pm onwards, Mon–Fri; From 2 pm onwards Sat–Sun

The optimal place to watch the cultural activities. Serves barbequed meats, salads and soups.

POOL AND CIGARS

40 50 04 36; From 5 pm onwards, Mon–Fri; from 2 pm onwards Sat–Sun

Pool hall, cocktail bar and tobacconist with direct access to the Soda Club at weekends.

SODA RESTAURANT AND CLUB
44 05 60 71; 10 am–12 am, Mon–Sun

This roomy, post-industrial-decor restaurant is always lively when
the concerts and films end, at around 10 pm. The small but quality
menu is 'New German Cuisine'; the restaurant also serves pizzas
and pancakes baked in the stone oven. The Soda Club upstairs
opens at 11 pm on Fri and Sat and caters for funky, glam tastes.

SOUND AND DRUMLAND
88 775 677, www.sound-and-drumland.de. 10 am–6.30 pm, Mon–Fri; 10 am–2 pm, Sat

Sound and Drumland has a vast selection of guitars, brass
instruments and electric keyboards; it's an industry favourite.

in the area

PRENZLAUERBERG
Zeiss Planetarium Prenzlauer Allee 80, 42 18 45 12, www.astw.de, 9
am–12 am, Mon–Fri; 7.30 pm–9 pm, Fri; 1.30 pm–9 pm, Sat; 1.30 pm–5
pm, Sun. Built in 1987, the planetarium with its 23-m dome boasts a
Cosmorama projector designed by Carl Zeiss. **Map p. 156, 2A**

FRIEDRICHSHAIN
East Side Gallery Mühlendamm 1.3-km stretch of wall whose east side
was decorated after 1989 by international peace campaigners. Tromp
d'oeil and kitsch graphics mythologise the wall, when what's really
impressive—and alarming—is its physical presence alone. **U** to
Warschauerstraße **Map p. 156, 2C**

Karl-Marx-Allee/Frankfurter Allee (formerly Stalinallee) The street was
built from the rubble of heavily-bombed Friedrichshain, and those who
built it were first on the list for housing on this new 'Socialist Boulevard'.
Now the entire street is a listed site that forms a vast, open-air
museum. Mid-Aug it's the site of the international beer festival, where
around two hundred breweries set up shop. Café Sybille is the original

The East Side Gallery

'*Milch Bar*', serving ice cream, milkshakes, coffee and cakes, and doubles as a museum of the history of the Allee. The star exhibit is the ear from the Stalin monument removed in 1961 at the start of the Brezhnev reforms; other exhibits include original architectural plans, photographic material of the 1953 uprising, and various consumer items from the GDR. Well worth a visit! *U* to Schillingstraße or Frankfurter Allee **Maps pp. 156, 1B, and 157, 1A**

Insel Stralau Peninsula with Spree views, where Karl Marx lived for a time as a student and now the site of some of Berlin's most sought-after property. Walk around the former glass factory, where the first trades union movement formed in Berlin, down towards the warehouse developments, boat clubs, nursery and park. Bus routes take you back up to Warschauer Straße. *U* to Warschauer Straße or Bus 147 **Map 157, 3A–3B**

Volkspark Friedrichshain Former flak emplacement and air-raid shelter, built by prisoners of war, and one of the last safe havens during Berlin's 'fall'. Climb the spiral path to the top for great views over the eastern half of the city. Also beach volleyball and an original GDR café in the summer. *S* to Landsberger Allee or Tram 5 or 6 **Map p. 156, 2B**

Corporate sponsorship and public art

All large-scale developments in Germany are obliged to put 1%–2% of their construction budget towards public art, a reintroduced piece of legislation from the Weimar Republic. In practice, the art produced has tended to represent the conservative tastes of the contractors.

Now light installations are ubiquitous: see Universal's illumination of their headquarters in the Spree Speicher, a former egg warehouse, and the next door Oberbaumbrücke, the mock-Gothic railway bridge built in 1902 and used during the wall-era as a footbridge between east and west. Also belonging to Universal is *13.4.1981* by **Olaf Metzel** (1987), a pile of police barricades. Formerly part of the Sculpture Boulevard in Charlottenburg (see p. 124), where it stood outside the entrance to U-bahn Joachimstalerstraße, the sculpture moved to the Spree Speicher in 2001. Metzel's inspiration came from an accidental sculpture 'created' during a demonstration following the announcement in the tabloid press of the death on a hunger strike of a leftwing terrorist. Further down-river is *Molecule Man* by **Jonathan Borofsky**, part of the Allianz art collection. The 30-m tall giant marks the intersection of Treptow, Friedrichshain and Kreuzberg.

FURTHER AFIELD
Off the map

Friedrichsfelde Cemetery Gudrunstraße. Open from 7.30 am, Feb–Nov; from 8 pm, Dec–Jan. 'The Socialist Cemetery' was founded in 1881. It has a memorial to the Revolution designed by Mies van der Rohe, and famous people buried there include Karl Liebknecht, Rosa Luxembourg, Frank Mehring, Erich Honecker, Käthe Kollwitz and Konrad Wolf. **U** or **S** to Lichtenberg, **S** to Friedrichsfelde-Ost, Bus 193 or Tram 21 or 27

Gedenkstätte Höhenschönhausen Genslerstraße 66, 98 60 82 30, www.gedenkstaette-hohenschonhausen.de. The former prison for political prisoners of the GDR regime; tours are given by former inmates (also in English). Unforgettable. **S** to Landsberger Allee, Tram 6, 7 or 17 to Genslerstraße stop

Jewish Cemetery Weißensee Markus-Reich-Platz 1, 925 33 30. In summer, 8 am–5 pm, Sun–Thur; In winter, 8 am–3 pm, Fri, 8 am–4 pm,

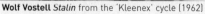

Wolf Vostell *Stalin* from the 'Kleenex' cycle (1962)

Sun–Thur. This is one of Europe's largest and most beautiful Jewish cemeteries, founded in 1880 when the community numbered 65,000 members. A grave containing the ashes of 809 Holocaust victims has a central position. Famous graves include Lesser Ury, Josef Bin Gorion and Max Hirsch. *U* to Shonhauser Allee, Tram 23 to the Herbert-Baum-Straße stop

galleries

Galerie Parterre Danziger Straße 101, 9 02 95 38 21, www.kulturamt-pankow.de. 2 pm–10 pm, Wed–Sun. Community gallery seeking to raise questions about the role of art in society through painting, drawing and sculpture. *U* to Eberswalderstraße **Map p. 156, 2A**

Galerie Vostell im Pfefferberg Schönhauser Allee 178, 885 22 80, www.vostell.de. 2 pm–6 pm, Tue–Sun. The gallery specialises in Fluxus artists including John Cage, Nam June Paik, Wolf Vostell (see picture) and Daniel Spoerri. Also shows younger artists following the Fluxus movement. **Map p. 156, 1B**

eat

PRENZLAUERBERG
RESTAURANTS

€ **Salamat** Duncker Straße 18, 444 31 36. Arab specialities with an Iraqi influence. There's a relaxed, friendly atmosphere and it's a popular lunch choice among local professionals. Falafal or haloumi costs €2.50, a soup €3.50. Meat and vegetables are served in clay pots with couscous for €6. *U* to Schönhauser Allee **Map p. 156, 1A**

Imbiss Salsabil Goehrenerstraße 6, 440 535 04. 11 am–12 am, Mon–Thur; 11 am–1 pm, Fri–Sun. Lebanese imbiss serving the best falafel on Helmholtzplatz. Also does Haloumi and Ma'an, all for €2.50. Help yourself to some well-stewed tea from the teapot in the corner. Favoured by workmen and academics alike. *U* to Eberswalderstraße **Map p. 156, 1A**

Wohnzimmer Lettestraße 6, 445 54 58. 10 am–4 pm. This aptly named café/bar is made up of cosy niches fitted out with big sofas, giving an appearance of cultivated decrepitude. They do an all-day breakfast and some tasty and cheap sandwiches. On summer afternoons, sit outside with the residents of the Helmholtzplatz, eat Apfeltorte and soak up the sunshine. A nearby playground provides diversion for the kinder. *U* to Eberswalder Straße/*S* to Schönhauser Allee **Map p. 156, 1A**

€€ **Kostbar** Knaackstraße 24, 43 73 55 74. This intimate café restaurant opposite the Wasserturm is a one-cook operation, with a menu that changes according to the season; in late spring asparagus features heavily, in summer it's chanterelle mushrooms, in winter it's duck with red cabbage. Soups, salads and rösti are on the menu all year round, backed up by a good wine list. Breakfast is served until 4 pm and cakes are delivered daily from a local baker. A local favourite. *U* to Eberswalder Straße **Map p. 156, 1A**

Prater Gaststätte & Biergarten Kastanienallee 7–9, 448 56 88, www.pratergarten.de. East Berlin's historic beer garden gets packed in the evenings. Grilled pork steaks, wurst and potato salad goes well with the beer. The rustic, wooden-fitted restaurant serves wholesome German cooking, and is a big favourite during the winter months. *U* to Eberswalderstraße **Map p. 156, 1A**

Urban Comfort Food Zionskirchstraße 5, 48 62 31 31. 12 pm–11 am, Mon–Thur; 12 pm–3 pm, Sat. Run by an engaged and international staff, the small, inventive and, above all, tasty menu changes every day. Watch the cook at work in the open-view kitchen—he may even be willing to take up pots and pans again should you arrive a little after eleven… Free entry to the disco downstairs if you've eaten at the restaurant. *U* to Rosenthaler Platz or Bernauer Straße **Map p. 9, 1A**

Soda Restaurant In the KulturBrauerei (see p. 165)

Voland Wichertstraße 63, 444 04 22. From 6 pm onwards. Authentic Russian restaurant serving excellent pelmini, blini and borscht, to be washed down with wines from Georgia and the Crimea, and

vodka by the carafe. Folk musicians on accordian and clarinet accompany the meal. Booking advised. *U* to Schönhauser Allee
Map p. 156, 1A

BARS

Haliflor Schwedter Straße 26, 547 133 11. 10 am–2 am, *U* to Eberswalder Straße. This café/bar a little way down the Kastanienallee is a good place to come after shopping. Big open windows looking onto the street make the bar nice and airy, while chanson and soul play in the background for atmosphere. Between smart and unkempt, the bar is the kind of cool, straightforward place it's hard to leave after just one drink. **Map p. 156, 1A**

Pfefferberg Schönhauser Allee 176, 44 38 33 42, www.pwag.net. Legendary venue and summer beer garden at the southernmost end of Prenzlauerberg, established back when ambient techno ruled the airwaves and Mitte was still a sandpit. *U* to Senerfelderplatz **Map p. 9, 2A**

Scotch and Sofa Kollwitzstraße 18, 44 04 23 71. This bar has got 1960s décor down to a tee. On Fridays and Saturdays DJs play pop, funk and soul. At the weekends it stays open until all the customers have gone home. Lots of snug seating and low tables. *U* to Senerfelderplatz **Map p. 9, 3A**

Torpedokäfer Dunckerstraße 69, 444 57 63. From 11 am onwards, Sun–Fri; from 4 pm onwards, Sat. This authentic drinkers' bar, popular with local artists, politicos and bohemians, has become a Prenzl'berg established establishment. Recommended. *U* to Prenzlauer Allee
Map p. 156, 1A

FRIEDRICHSHAIN
RESTAURANTS AND BARS

Dachkammer Simon-Dach-Straße 39, 296 16 73. Walking into this cosy, wood-panelled bar restaurant, you wouldn't believe there's a chic cocktail lounge upstairs. The best on Friedrichshain's bar strip. *U* to Frankfurter Tor **Map p. 157, 2B**

Zur Glühlampe Lehmbruckstraße 1, www.zurgluehlampe.de. From 4 pm onwards. Renovated Eck-Kneipe on the south side of the railway track, with reggae and ska and techno DJs every day of the week (except Mon). Look in if you're visiting Intershop2000 (see p. 175). *U* to Warschauer Straße **Map p. 157, 2B**

Volkswirtschaft Krossener Straße 17, www.volkswirtschaft.de. A place to find quality, yet inexpensive health food; the atmosphere is lo-fi, with all the furniture taken from second-hand shops and the owners' friends' flats. *U* to Frankfurter Tor **Map p. 157, 2B**

shop

PRENZLAUERBERG

CLOTHES AND SHOES

Calypso Oderberger 61, 281 61 65, www.calypso-shoes.com. Open afternoons. From clogs to cowboy boots, flip-flops to platforms, this is the place to find both second-hand and unworn shoes from the 1950s to the 1990s. There's a second shop at Rosenthaler Straße 23. A must for shoe fanatics. *U* to Eberswalderstraße **Map p. 156, 1A**

Eisdieler Kastanienallee 12, 285 73 51. Open afternoons. A Berlin designers' collective, featuring colourful, humorous and experimental clothes for street and clubwear. Women are well catered for, with labels including Stylvant, Schmoove and presque fini, while Director's Cut sorts out the men with natty numbers such as the suit in imitation snakeskin. One of the best on Prenzl'berg's fashion strip. *U* to Eberswalderstraße **Map p. 156, 1A**

East Berlin Kastienhalle 13, 534 40 42, www.eastberlin.net. Open afternoons. A Berlin label whose philosophy is 'to capture the feel of life and love in the capital'; T-shirts are printed with the Fernsehturm or modified BRD crests. Occasionally runs unusual deals, such as 'buy a bag and get a free ticket to the opera'. Fashion full of intriguing contradictions, like Berlin itself. *U* to Eberswalderstraße **Map p. 156, 1A**

Hasipop Shop Oderberger 39, 44 03 34 91, www.hasipop.de. Open afternoons. For bunny girls with scores to settle, Hasipop combines cute with mean. Characteristic are the T-shirts with the Fernsehturm, a toothey, eyeless smiley-face. The shop is also a

shop!

record label for local producers, and on the scene it's the girls who are running things. *U* to Eberswalderstraße **Map p. 156, 1A**

Hit-In.TV Oderberger Straße 37, 97 00 47 20, www.hit-in.tv. A gem of a label, with bright, retro, folklore styles in floral patterns and canvas. The owner describes it as 'Granny to Rock and Roll': a qualified graphic designer, she learned stitching from her grandmother. She specialises in women's jackets, skirts and bags; customers can choose a material, which she will then tailor into a personalised design. *U* to Eberswalderstraße **Map p. 156, 1A**

Sgt. Peppers Kastanienallee 91/92, 448 11 21. 11 am–7.30 pm, Mon–Fri; 11 am–4 pm, Sat. Carefully selected second-hand clothing from the 1950s to the 1970s, specialising in women's wear. A great range of all-in-one numbers in stretchy polyester. Also big billowy frocks. New dresses and pool wear produced under the Sgt. Peppers label include great bold designs as well as delicate paisleys. Everything at reasonable prices. *U* to Eberswalderstraße **Map p. 156, 1A**

Thatchers Kastanienallee 21, 24 62 77 51, www.thatchers.de. Open afternoons. This famed Berlin label for women was established in 1994. Their home is in Prenzl'berg, but they've since opened outlets in Mitte (Hackescher Hof) and Paris. The label's success lies in its minimalism; Thatchers seems almost monochrome alongside other labels. The Bauhaus aesthetic is evident in the combination of classic and modern styles. *U* to Eberswalderstraße **Map p. 156, 1A**

MARKET

Flöhmarkt am Arkonaplatz 93 79 87 55. 10 am–5 pm, Sun. Flea market of choice: it might be junk, but it's junk from Prenzlauerberg. *U* to Bernauerstrasse

GIFTS

In't Veld Schokoladen Dunckerstraße 10, 48 62 34 23, www.intveld.de. Open afternoons. Chocolate imported from the countries of origin at prices not that much higher than the mass-produced brands. And these sweets are so rich, you don't want to eat the whole bar in one go. *U* to Eberswalderstraße **Map p. 156, 1A**

Luxus International Kastanienallee 101, 44 32 48 77. 11 am–8 pm, Mon–Fri; 11 am–4 pm, Sat. A forum for young international product designers. From bags to t-shirts and cards: the common feature is that everything is imaginative and humorous. A first stop for a cheap and amusing present. *U* to Eberswalderstraße **Map p. 156, 1A**

FRIEDRICHSHAIN

Berlinomat Frankfurt Allee 89, 420 81 445, www.berlinomat.com. 11
am–8 pm, Mon–Fri; 10–16, Sat. Halfway up the Franfurter Allee, in
the heart of East Berlin, between discount stores and shopping
arcades, is Berlin's trendiest and most progressive shop. Founded
in 2003, Berlinomat offers retailing and marketing services to the
100 or so designers whose products it features in its large, airy
rooms. All products must have a concept and be made in Berlin.
Labels to look out for are East Berlin, Milk and Hasipop, while for
shoes, check the Zeha trainers: they're the authentic GDR brand,
updated but retaining the original design. Also good is the
wallpaper from Xtratapete: rolls of jungle vegetation, palm fronds
and alpine meadows. (There is a café in-house, too.) Experience
what's being hailed as the future of retailing in the capital. *U* to
Frankfurter Allee **Map p. 157, 1A**

East of Eden Schreinerstraße 10, 423 93 62, www.east-of-eden.de. Open
afternoons. Looking for TS Eliot in Turkish, Chomsky in Finnish, or
an anthology of modern Monogolian poetry? East of Eden is wall-
to-wall with second-hand and antiquarian books in most European
languages. The emphasis is on books in English, which they import
from the UK; they also take books on an exchange. At regular
intervals, musicians (not unknown to aficionados of formative
punk) climb onto the small stage out back, play, get drunk and fall
back off. Run by a friendly bunch of expats from the UK and US. *U*
to Frankfurter Tor **Map p. 157, 1B**

Intershop2000 Ehrenbergstr 3–7, 31 80 03 64, www.intershop2000-
berlin.de. 2 pm–6 pm, Wed–Fri; 12 pm–6 pm, Sat; 12.30 pm–6 pm,
Sun. A brilliant anachronism. Next door to Friedrichshain's office
complex is a low, long, prefab building of a type mass-produced in
the GDR between 1960 and 1975. It houses Intershop2000, which
calls itself 'The Shop Window of the East', an exhibition, retail and
exchange point for everything related to GDR consumer culture.
Stackable plastic cutlery; socialist youth scout regalia; Russian
comics; Vita Cola; books on Marxist economic theory; and posters
of the pop group 'Die Puhdys'. Intershop2000 seems permanently
on the point of disappearing into a time warp. *U* to Warschauerstraße or Schlesiches Tor **Map p. 157, 3B**

Trödelmarkt am Boxhagener Platz 0177 827 93 52; 9 am–4 pm, Sat–Sun.
Friedrichshainers never miss this weekly market, which
specialises in household items from the eastern half of the city. *U*
to Frankfurter Tor **Map p. 157, 2B**

entertainment

INFORMATION
TICKETS
VENUES
NIGHTLIFE
TOURS
FESTIVALS
SPORT
THEATRES

WHERE TO GET INFORMATION

The reigning English-language paper for Berlin is the *ExBerliner*, which costs €2 and is published once a month. It has music, entertainment, film and restaurant listings, interviews and opinion pieces, and can be purchased at newsstands, cafés, cinemas and bookstores around the city.

If you are undaunted by umlauts, try the more comprehensive *Zitty* or *Tip*, published on alternate Wednesdays.

Exberliner www.ex-berliner.de

Zitty www.zitty.de

Tip www.berlinonline.de/tip

WHERE TO BUY TICKETS
IN PERSON

Most venues have a box office; ticket agencies charge a handling fee. For the larger concert halls, you can buy tickets online, directly from their websites, for a smaller fee. Discounted tickets are available to students and seniors at the Deutsche Oper, the Staatsoper and the Komische Oper on the day of the show, one hour before the performance.

TICKET AGENCIES

Ticket agencies can be found in larger department stores, such as **Galeria Kaufhof** (Alexanderplatz; Map p. 9, 2B), **Karstadt** (Hermann Platz; Map p. 133, 2C), **Wertheim** (Tauentziehenstraße; Map p. 105, 2C) and **KaDeWe** (Wittenberg Platz; Map p. 105, 3C).

You can also try **Ars Scribendi**, on the top floor of the Potsdamer Platz Arkaden at Alte Potsdamer Straße 7 (Map p. 8, 2C). **Hekticket** at Hardenbergstrasse 2, 230 9930, (Map p. 105, 1B) sells last minute half-price tickets.

VENUES
THEATRE, OPERA AND DANCE

Peformances at the major opera houses and concert halls unsually start at 7.30 pm. Check in advance through the websites or ticket hotlines for availability, accesibility, and discounts. See the Berliner Bühne posters in S and U-bahn stations for current programme listings, but bear in mind that most ensembles are on leave in August.

THEATRE

Berliner Ensemble Bertoldt Brecht Platz, 284 08155. Bertoldt Brecht's Threepenny Opera was first performed in this lavish baroque building in 1928, and Brecht directed the Ensemble starting from 1949 until his death in 1956. The current director, Claus Peymann, has balanced tastefully the demands of political theater with contemporary aesthetics. *U* or *S* to Friedrichstrasse **Map p. 8, 3B**

Friends of the Italian Opera Fidicinstraße 40, Tel: 691 12 11. Stages a wide variety of English-language theatre, including works by young contemporary playwrights. *U* to Platz der Luftbrücke **Map p. 132, 2C**

Maxim Gorki Theater Am Festungsgraben 2, 20 221 115. Small theater on Unter den Linden designed by Schinkel, used in the GDR for productions by Maxim Gorky and contemporary Eastern Bloc playwrights. The company puts on new works as well as modern classics and has continued to showcase theatre from Eastern Europe. *S* or *U* to Friedrichstraße **Map p. 8, 3B**

Volksbühne Rosa-Luxemburg-Platz, 247 6772. This is Berlin's premier avant-garde theater, and productions are often sold out weeks in advance. Also home to the Röter Salon, a bar that has readings and DJs playing funk, pop and soul, decorated in chandeliers and red velvet, and to the Grüner Salon, with a green theme and swing and Latin dancing. *U* to Rosa-Luxemburg-Platz **Map p. 9, 2A**

OPERA

Deutsche Oper Bismarkstrasse 35, 343 84 01, www.deutscheoper berlin.de. Founded in 1907 as an alternative to the aristocratic Royal Opera House (now the Staatsoper), the 'people's opera' is currently housed in a brick-and-glass block. *U* to Deutsche Oper or Bismarckstraße **Map p. 104, 3B**

Komische Oper Unter den Linden 41, 4799 7400, www.komische-oper-berlin.de. Major institution for opera, dance and musical theater known for its dramatic set design. *S* or *U* to Friedrichsstraße **Map p. 8, 3B**

Staatsoper Unter den Linden 7, 030 20 35 40, www.staatsoper-berlin.org. A beautiful space, originally built in 1742 and reconstructed after World War II. Don't miss the delicious cake in the luxurious basement cafe. *U* or *S* Friedrichstraße **Map p. 8, 3B**

DANCE

Both the Staatsoper and the Komische Oper have ballet programs. Also look out for the 'Tanz in August' series in the summer, which brings modern dance composers from around the world to Berlin for three exhaustive weeks of modern dance.

Dock 11 Kastanienallee 79, 448 1222, www.dock11-berlin.de. Workspaces, studios and stages for working choreographers. Regularly showcases work by artists-in-residence and smaller dance companies. *U* to Eberswalderstraße **Map p. 156, 1A**

Podewil Klosterstraße 68-70, 247 49 6, www.podewil.de. Well-known contemporary performance space in the heart of Berlin, with programming devoted to modern dance. *U* to Klosterstraße **Map p. 9, 2B**

MUSIC
CLASSICAL MUSIC

Berliner Philharmonie Herbert von Karajan Strasse 1, 254 88 999, www.berliner-philharmoniker.de. Even if it weren't the home of the world-renowed Berlin Philharmonic, it would be worth a trip for the architecture alone, a classic 1960s design by Hans Scharoun. The stage is built like a podium around which the seats are arranged and the gilded exterior is finished in a series of flourishes. The Philharmonic is directed by Sir Simon Rattle. *U* or *S* to Potsdamer Platz **Map p. 69, 2C**

Haus der Berliner Festspiele
Schaperstraße 24, 254 890, www.berliner festspiele.de. Off map. This swanky wood and glass music hall around the corner from the University of Arts shows primarily new music. *U* to Spichernstraße

Konzerthaus
Gendarmenmarkt, 20 30 90. Originally designed by Karl Friedrich Schinkel in 1818 to replace the National Theater, which had burned down. His plan was sensational, creating a new kind of space by

Potsdamer Platz

construcing a lower and broader proscenium in place of the usual high baroque stage. The result, with its teardrop chandeliers, is gorgeous. It is now home to the Berliner Sinfonie-Orchester (BSO) under the leadership of conductor Eliahu Inbal. *U* to Französischestraße **Map p. 8, 3C**

JAZZ
A-Trane Bleibtreustraße 1 at Pestalozzistraße, 313 25 50. If you go, reserve a table at this posh club showcasing international and local bebop, swing and cool jazz acts. *S* to Savignyplatz **Map p. 105, 1C**

Quasimodo Kantstr. 12a, 312 80 86, www.quasimodo.de. Berlin's oldest jazz club. The best-of-the-best have played here deep into smoke-filled nights since 1975. *S* or *U* to Zoologischer Garten **Map p. 105, 2C**

Soultrane Kantstraße 17, 315 1860. An American-style dining club that draws big-name acts. Has in the past hosted Herbie Hancock, Ute Lemper, Till Brönner, Joe Lovano, Diana Krall and Brad Mehldau. **Map p. 105, 1C**

Schlot Chausseestraße 18, 448 21 60, www.kunstfabrik-schlot.de. A spot favouring free and improvised jazz is in the basement of a converted factory. *U* to Zinnowitzerstraße **Map p. 8, 3A**

Zosch Tucholskystraße 30, 280 76 64. One of the first cafés to open in Mitte after the Berlin Wall came down, and one of the few still left standing. Rustic and almost always busy; jazz bands often play in its basement. *S* to Oranienburgerstraße **Map p. 9, 1B**

ROCK AND POP

Ausland Lychener Straße 60, 44 77 008, www.ausland-berlin.de. Minimalist cube tucked into a rock'n'roll facade close to Helmholtz Platz, the heart of hip Prenzlauerberg. The music is eclectic, ranging from music concret and new music to post-punk electrorock. *S* or *U* to Schönhauser Allee **Map p. 156, 1A**

Nbi Schönhauser Allee 157, 4405 1681. The 'new Berlin initiative' represents the best in local electronic music, with its own label and a comfortable 1970s style lounge. *U* to Eberswalderstraße **Map p. 156, 1A**

Kurvenstar Kleine Präsidentenstraße 24 723 115, www.kurvenstar.de. Trendy Hackescher Markt club showcasing good hip-hop acts. The website is worth a visit in itself. *S* or *U* to Hackescher Markt **Map p. 9, 1B**

Tempodrom Askanischer Platz 4, 263 998 0, www.tempodrom-berlin.de. Paragon of post-wall Berliner architecture and a major venue for rock shows. Beneath is the 'liquidrom', a salt water spa featuring underwater music. *U* to Anhalter Bahnhof **Map p. 132, 2B**

SO36 Oranienstraße 190, 030 6140 1306. West Berlin's answer to CBGB—hard core and hip-hop, with a bit of straight edge and disco thrown in. Transvestite bingo on Mon nights. *U* to Kottbusser Tor **Map p. 133, 2B**

Supamolly Jessenerstraße 41, 2900 7294, www.supamolly.de. *East* Berlin's answer to CBGB—punky, political, grungy, with a bar upstairs and a stage in the basement. *U* or *S* to Frankfurter Allee **Map p. 105, 3A**

Wild At Heart Wiener Straße, 030 611 70 10. Good rock at a low prices; the place to soak up a bit of timeless hippie-anarchist Kreuzberg flavour. *U* to Görlitzer Bahnhof **Map p. 157, 3C**

FOLK AND WORLD MUSIC

Haus der Kulturen der Welt John Foster Dulles Allee 10 (in the Tiergarten). Host to world music concerts by top international acts. *S* to Unter den Linden, then Bus 100 **Map 8, 1B**

Werkstatt der Kulturen Wissmannstraße 32, 6097 700. The organisers of the Carnival der Kulturen parade host a work and presentation space for immigrant arts. *U* to Hermannplatz **Map p. 133, 2C**

CLUBS

Maria am Ufer Stralauer Platz 34/35. Progressive experimental music: come here to hear genres someone created that morning. *S* to Ostbahnhof **Map p. 157, 3B**

Mudd Club Große Hamburgerstraße. 17, 4403 6299, www.muddclub-berlin.de. Billed as the successor to the legendary New York punk/no wave club, combines music with performance art; also poetry readings with theme party happenings. Authenticity provided by Steven Mass, the name behind both the original and the new Mudds. *S* to Oranienburgerstraße **Map p. 9, 1B**

Icon Cantianstraße. 15, 4849 2878. London meets Berlin in this club devoted to breakbeat and drum 'n' bass; light installations surround the dancefloor. *U* to Eberswalderstraße **Map p. 156, 1A**

Sage Köpenickerstraße 76, 27 89 83 0. Built into the basement of a Metro station, Sage reanimates the extravagance and excess of the club scene of fifteen years ago. *U* to Heinrich-Heine-Straße **Map p. 9, 3C**

Tresor Leipziger Straße 126a, 52 94 85 284. Devoted to "pure underground techno" since the day it opened in 1991 in a former department store vault and air raid shelter. Has its own label, Tresor Records. *S* or *U* to Potsdamer Platz **Map p. 132, 2A**

WMF Karl Marx Allee 34, www.wmfclub.de. A club spinning rare funk, electro, and hip hop and house. Venue subject to change, but currently located at Cafe Moskau on Frankfurter Allee. *U* to Schillingstraße **Map p. 9, 3B**

CINEMA

Most movies are dubbed into German. When looking for English-language movies, make sure to that "OV" (original version) or "OmU" (original with subtitles) next to the title in the listings.

Babylon Berlin Dresdenerstraße 126, 6160 9693 Tucked away in a side street near Kottbusser Tor, this cozy theatre shows the latest British and American independent releases. A great place to catch an evening flick before hitting the Kreuzberg bar scene. Möbel Olfe, in the cul-de-sac at the end of the street, is the place to kick off a post-cinema pub crawl. *U* Kottbusser Tor **Map p. 133, 1A**

Cinema Paris Berlin Kurfürstendamm, 8813119. The place to see French-language films in Berlin, usually with German subtitles. *S* to Savignyplatz, *U* to Uhlandstraße **Map p. 105, 1C**

Cinestar im Sony Center Potsdamerstraße 4, 260 66 400. A cavernous multiplex offering high-budget Hollywood releases in English with German subtitles. *S* or *U* to Potsdamer Platz **Map p. 8, 2C**

Fsk am Oranienplatz Segitzdamm 2, 614 2464. Small Kreuzberg cinema screens independent foreign films in original language. *U* to Kottbusser Tor **Map p. 133, 1B**

Hackesche Hof Rosenthalerstraße 40/41, 283 4603. In the 1990s the Hackesche Hof morphed from a semi-delapidated squat into a highbrow leisure establishment; go there to shop, eat, drink coffee, listen to street musicians, watch cabaret or catch a movie in English. *S* to Hackescher Markt, *U* to Weinmeisterstraße **Map p. 9, 1B**

High End 54 Tacheles, Oranienburgerstraße. 54-56, 283 1498. Located on the second floor of an artists' studio building, High End shows indie and art films in spartan surroundings. The smokey foyer doubles as a laid-back lounge done in minimalist red velvet cubes. *U* to Oranienburger Tor, *S* to Oranienburgerstraße **Map p. 9, 1B**

Odeon Berlin Hauptstraße 116, 7870 4019. Off map. Large, old, single-screen cinema in Schöneberg in West Berlin showing foreign films in the orginal language. *S* to Schöneberg

planning

WHEN TO GO
HOW TO GET AROUND
PRACTICALITIES
FOOD AND DRINK
PLACES TO STAY

WHEN TO GO

Like all of Europe, May–Sept is the most popular tourist season and the time of year when the city takes to the streets (it can rain in summer, though). Winter and early spring bring grey skies and cold temperatures, but fewer visitors.

PASSPORTS AND FORMALITIES

No visas are needed when travelling from within the EU, though passports are still checked if you are coming from the UK or new member states. US nationals are not required to have a visa for stays of less than three months, but travellers from the US with no return ticket are not allowed into Germany. All German nationals are legally required to carry an ID card at all times; it is a good idea to keep your passport on you should you need to provide ID, for example when paying with a credit card.

GETTING THERE
BY AIR

Two airports serve Berlin: **Tegel** in the north west and **Schönefeld** in the south east (for info on either, 01805 00 01 86).

LOCAL NUMBERS
British Airways 01805 266 522
Easy Jet 01 803 654 321
Air Berlin 01805 73 78 00
Ryanair 01 90 170 100 (Mon–Fri)

BY TRAIN FROM THE UK

The Eurostar can be taken from Waterloo to Brussels, where you can pick up the ICE (Intercity Express) to Berlin. www.bahn.de.

BY CAR

Berlin can be reached from Hannover on the E30, from Dresden on the E55, and from Hamburg on the E26.

The E55 circles Berlin. Take exit 11 to the 133 and exit 1 at Treptow to approach from the south; exit 26 at Spandau from the west; or exit 35 at Pankow from the north.

Parking is metered in central areas of Mitte and Charlottenburg, and there is a pay carpark in Potsdamer Platz. A good bet for spaces is along the Straße der 17 Juni, providing the road hasn't been closed off for demonstrations or other events.

GETTING TO THE CITY CENTRE

From Tegel airport, takes the 128 bus to Kurt-Schumacher-Platz, then take the U6 south to Friedrichstraße. Allow at least 45 minutes for the journey.

From Schönefeld, take the S9 or the Regional Bahn (no travel cards) to Friedrichstraße. Allow at least an hour for the return journey—trains don't run all that frequently so it's worth checking the timetable first. A warning: the S45 ring train may have Schönefeld as its final destination, but it goes in an anti-clockwise direction and may not be the fastest train. Your best bet is to go to Treptower Park and then take the S9.

A taxi from Tegel to Friedrichstraße should cost you about €17, from Schönefeld to Friedrichstraße about €26 (26 10 26).

GETTING AROUND

Berlin is well linked up by public transportation—U-bahn, S bahn, bus and tram—all run by Berliner Verkehrsbetrieb (BVG). The S-bahn ring goes in both directions and is quicker than the U-bahn over long distances (the S 5-7-9 through the city is the quickest east-west connection). The tram covers eastern Berlin and some parts of the west.

TICKETS

Tickets are sold by zones:
Zone A is inside the ring,
Zone B within city borders,
Zone C includes
Brandenburg. Unless you
want to go to Potsdam, you
are safe with just the AB
ticket.

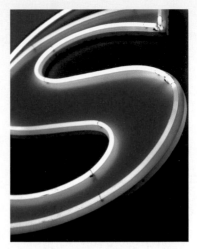

Information is available at
platforms (though not
necessarily in English). U-
bahn ticket counters are
usually open 5.30 am–8.30
pm (at 4.15 pm on
weekends).

The U-bahn usually stops
running just after midnight
and starts again at 3 am, except on weekends, where most lines
run all night.

Always stamp your ticket before travelling!

TYPES OF TICKET

Kurze Strecke Valid for 3 stations on the U/S, 6 stations on bus or tram:
€1.20/€1

Standard fare for Berlin (Zone AB) Valid for 2 hours, can't be used for
return or round journeys; single-fare ticket: €2/€1.50

Day ticket Valid until 3 pm the day after stamping: €5.60/€4.20

Group ticket (Zone AB) Valid until 3 pm the day after stamping: €14 for up
to five persons

7-Day Ticket (Zone AB) €24.30

Welcome Card (Zone ABC) Valid for 72 hours, for one adult and three
children, with reductions on museums and city tours: €21

GUIDED TOURS

The Insider Tour www.insidertour.com. Quick and light hearted tours
meet daily at 10 am and 2.30 pm at the Zoologischer Garten station and

10 am and 3 pm at Hackescher Markt (in Apr–Oct and Nov–Mar mornings tours only).

Brewer's Best of Berlin www.brewersberlin.com. Highly informative tours for €10. Meet at the New Synagogue on Oranienburgerstraße at 10.30 am and 12.30 pm.

BOAT TRIPS

Stern und Kreis 53 63 60 0, www.sternundkreis.de. The daily three-hour tour (Apr–Oct) is €10 one way, €15 return, English commentary on request.

MONEY

Cash machines aren't all that common, especially out of the centre, but Berliner Sparkasse is the most ubiquitous. All cash machines accept Visa, EC and Mastercard debit and credit cards, and charge a fee of around €3.50 for all foreign transactions.

Banks are open 9 am–6 pm, Tue and Thur; 9 am–3 pm Mon and Wed; and 9 am–1 pm, Fri.

It's a good idea to carry cash with you, as many restaurants don't accept cards. All banks exchange currency, and there are bureaux de change at Alexanderplatz and Zoologischer Garten.

WEB RESOURCES

www.exberliner.com English language magazine with listings

www.smart-travelling.net online travel guide

www.berliner-galerien.de independent art galleries

www.kurfuerstendamm.de guide to Berlin's shopping mile

www.smb.spk-berlin.de central state museum site

www.bvg.de public transport in the city

www.tip-berlin.de entertainment listings, in German

INFORMATION OFFICES

Berlin Tourist Information (walk-in, no phone service) Brandenburger Tor, south wing. Open daily, 9.30 am–6 pm. **Map p. 8, 2B**

MUSEUM PASSES
STATE MUSEUMS

SMB (Staatliche Museen Berlin) museums are divided into zones. You cannot buy a ticket for an individual museum, but only for all museums in that zone for one day. Children under16 enter free and there are reductions for students, the unemployed and the disabled. There is free entry every Thur, four hours before closing. 2090 55 66, www.smpk.de

Museumsinsel (Alte Nationalgalerie, Alte Museum, Pergamon Museum) €8/€4

Tiergarten (Neue Nationalgalerie permanent collection, Gemäldegalerie, Hamburger Bahnhof) €6/€3

Charlottenburg (Sammlung Berggruen, Museum für Fotografie, Ägyptisches Museum, Museum für Vor- und Frühgeschichte, Bröhan Museum) €6/€3

Day ticket to all Staatliche Museen Berlin museums €10/€5; three-day ticket €12/€6

Schloß Charlottenberg belongs to the SPSG (Stiftung Preußischer Schlößer und Gärten). A two-day ticket (€12/€9) gives entry to all buildings, including Potsdam. 320 91 1, www.spsg.de

TELEPHONE AND POSTAL SERVICES
TELEPHONE
Dialling code for Germany 0049
Dialling code for Berlin (0) 30
Local directory enquiries in English 11837
Foreign directory enquiries 11834
Operator 0180 200 1033

Public telephones are recognisable by the illuminated pink signs. Telephone cards can be brought in newsagents and kiosks.

POST OFFICES
Mitte Georgenstraße 12 (*S* or *U* to Friedrichstraße). Open 6 am–10 pm, Mon–Fri; 8 am–10 pm, Sat–Sun **Map p. 8, 3B**

Tiergarten Potsdamerstraße 134–136 (*U* to Potsdamerplatz). 8.30 am–6.30 pm, Mon–Fri; 9.30 am–1.30 pm, Sat **Map p. 68, 1C**

Charlottenburg Joachimstalerstraße 7 (*U* to Zoologischer Garten). Open 9 am–8 pm, Mon–Fri **Map p. 105, 2C**

Kreuzberg Hallesches Ufer 60 (*U* to Hallesches Tor). 8 am–6.30 pm, Mon–Fri; 8.30 am–1 pm, Sat **Map p. 132, 2B**

INTERNET ACCESS
Mitte
Kaufhof am Alexanderplatz (*U* to Alexanderplatz) **Map p. 9, 2B**
Kultur Kaufhaus Friedrichstraße (*U* to Friedrichstraße) **Map p. 8, 3B**
C@ll shop Brunnenstraße 5 (*U* to Rosenthalerplatz) **Map p. 9, 1A**
Kreuzberg
@-Friends Bergmann Straße 97 (*U* to Gneisenau Straße) **Map p. 132, 2C**
Internet & Telecafe Hallesches Ufer 24 (*U* to Hallesches Tor) **Map p. 132, 2B**
Wiener Teleshop Wienerstraße 9 (*U* to Görlitzer Bahnhof) **Map p. 132, 2B**
Charlottenburg
Log-in-Café Knesebeckstraße 38–49 (*U* to Uhlandstraße) **Map p. 105, 1C**

EMERGENCIES AND PERSONAL SECURITY
TELEPHONE
Police 110
Fire/ambulance 112
24-hour medical 31 00 31
Directory enquiries in English 11 8 37
BVG (public transport) 19 44 9
Funk Taxi Berlin 26 10 26
English crisis line (6 pm–12 am) 44 01 06 07

EMBASSIES
UK Wilhelmstraße 70, 204 570 **Map p. 8, 3B**
US Neustädtische Kirchstraße 4–5, 238 51 47 **Map p. 8, 3B**
Ireland Friedrichstraße 200, 220 720 **Map p. 8, 3C**
Australia Friedrichstraße 200, 88 00 88 0 **Map p. 8, 3C**
New Zealand Friedrichstraße 60, 206 210 **Map p. 8, 3C**
Canada Friedrichstraße 95, 203 120 **Map p. 8, 3C**

HEALTH
MAIN HOSPITAL
Charitee Hospital Schumannstraße 20/21, 450 50,
www.charitee.de **Map p. 8, 2B**

CHEMISTS
In each region, at least two chemists are open until 10 pm and two
are open all night. This is done on a rotation schedule. To find out,
call the 24-hour emergency medical service at 31 00 31.

LOST PROPERTY
BVG lost property office Potsdamerstraße 180/182, 25 62 30 40
Central Lost Property Office Platz der Luftbrücke 6, 6 99 5

DISABLED TRAVELLERS
There are lifts for wheelchair users in U-bahn and S-bahn
stations, as well as ramps for boarding S-bahn trains at the front
of each carriage (ask the platform manager).
   All museums have ramps and lifts; check with the museum in
advance for more extensive needs.

FOOD AND DRINK
RESTAURANT PRICE GUIDE
€ = under €10 per head
€€ = between €10 and €20 per head
€€€ = over €20 per head

RESTAURANT ETIQUETTE AND TIPPING

After a meal the waiter or waitress will ask *'Hat's geschmeckt?'*, or
'did it taste good?', for which the stock reply is *'Ja danke'*. You can
then add, *'die Rechnung, bitte'* ('the bill please'). The waitress will
assume you are paying *'zusammen'* (together) unless you say
'getrennt bitte' (separate, please).
   Service is very rarely included in restaurant bills, but tipping is
expected: around 10% is usual. The tip should be given to the
waiter or waitress and not left on the table—telling him or her the
total you wish to pay suffices.

In bars table service is the norm, and buying drinks at the bar to take to your seat is unheard of. Don't be surprised if the waitress knocks on the table: this means '*Prost*' (cheers). You pay for all drinks at the end (they may have been marked them off on a beer mat). Tipping in bars is more flexible, though rounding the amount up is always appreciated. It's a good way to be wished '*Einen schönen Abend noch*' ('have a nice evening').

CITY FOODS

Menus are usually straightforward, especially if you speak a bit of German, but below are some foods beloved of Berliners that you might not otherwise know about.

Berliner Bock—a beer brewed a little bit stronger than regular pils

Boulette—a meatball with French origins, served cold in a Belegte Brötchen (open sandwich)

Currywurst—chopped up Bratwurst with curry powder and ketchup (most people eat it standing, on the way to or from work)

Döner—You can have your kebab sandwich '*mit alles?*' (salad?), '*Welche*

Soße?' (garlic or spicy sauce?) and *'einpacken oder gleich essen?'* (wrapped or open?).

Glühwein mit Schuß—Glühwein with a shot of rum

Hefeweizen—Bavarian beer brewed from wheat, either *hell* (light), *dunkel* (dark) or *kristall* (clear)

Königsburger Klopse—meat balls in a cream and lemon sauce

Pommes Rotweiss—chips with ketchup and mayonnaise

Schrippen—a bread roll best eaten fresh from the oven.

Spargel—white asparagus. They are in season around May

Stollen—Christmas current loaf with a marzipan (West German) or poppy seed (East German) filling

TEA AND COFFEE

Germany takes its coffee seriously—evidenced by the absence of instant coffee on supermarket shelves—and most Germans drink about a litre of it every morning. The coffee is twice-roasted and therefore tends to be bitter. Black coffee is *'schwarze Kaffee'* and a latte is a *'Milchcafé'*.

If coffee is the office worker's poison of choice, tea is seen as mind- and body-enhancing. There are hundreds of varieties of herbal and fruit teas, such as *'Jogi Tee'*, renowned for its relaxant effect. If you want an English cuppa ask for *'Schwarzen Tee'*, though be prepared for funny looks if you add milk.

Smoking

In Berlin smoking is a demonstration of an inalienable personal freedom, and even non-smokers are pro-smoking. Ask someone whether they mind if you smoke and they're likely to tell you no, they don't, and this isn't California. On the other hand, exercise your right not to inhale someone else's smoke and people will think you're uptight. A recent attempt to introduce the EU ban on smoking in bars and restaurants was a complete failure: bar-owners were aghast, smokers righteous and non-smokers worried about losing their drinking partners. However, U-bahn platforms banned smoking a few years back.

OPENING HOURS

State museums are open 10 am–6 pm, Tue–Sun, and 10 am–10 pm, Thur. They are closed Mondays. For other museums see individual listings.

Shops open at 9.30 am and close at 6 pm, though bigger shops and supermarkets stay open later. On Saturday everything shuts down at 1 pm. Restaurants usually serve food until around midnight; bars close at around 1 am during the week and 4 pm at weekends, though some stay open all night.

PUBLIC HOLIDAYS IN BERLIN

January	New Year's Day
March	Good Friday
March/April	Easter
May	May Day (May 1st); Ascension Day; Pentecost
October	Reunification day
December	Christmas, Boxing Day

ART CALENDER

Biennale International Contemporary art, Feb–April, www.berlin biennale.de

Berlinale International film festival, Feb. www.berlinale.de

Bread & Butter Berlin International fashion show, Jan. www.bread andbutter.com

Long Night of the Museums Jan and Aug. One ticket (€12/€8) allows access to as many museums as it is possible to see in one night (between 6 pm and 2 am); museums put on concerts, light shows, tours, buffets, film evenings and discos. A bus service, included in the ticket price, shuttles visitors along six possible routes. www.lange-nacht-der-museen.de

Transmediale Digital art and media event, Jan. www.trans mediale.de

Tag der Öffenen Turen Second to last weekend in August (subject to change). Open house day to government buildings otherwise closed to the public, including the Chancellery and the Town Hall. With shuttle service. www.bundesregierung.de

Berliner Mode

On first impressions, Berlin may not seem to be a fashion city, but look under the surface and you'll find Berliner Mode is booming.

Berlin's reputation as a youth-oriented, club culture city is reflected in current design trends. The trademark style is a trashy, ironic look that draws on the West Berlin punk and art-rock scene of the 1970s and 1980s (this is the unifying theme for fun, clever and outrageous labels like Killer Beast, East Berlin and Hasipop).

Other designers take a more functionalist approach, based on distinctive elements of Berlin's design history. Some are influenced by Bauhaus (Thatchers), or draw on the golden 1920s era (Fiona Bennett's hats). The Universität der Kunst runs Berlin's top fashion design programme (led by Vivienne Westwood). The proliferation of small labels—with one or two stores and an internet presence—is due in part to the influence of the school, and to the fact that many Berlin-trained designers have stayed in the city after graduating.

Berlin's claim to being Germany's alternative fashion centre has been boosted by the annual 'Bread and Butter Berlin' show, now in its fourth year. Interior design is also booming. Furniture is minimalist, with a 1970s flavour, purpose-made for the spacious interiors available to middle-income brackets. An important initiative for launching young Berlin designers has been the Berlinomat network, whose shop in Friedrichshain showcases over a hundred local innovators. All products are sold on commission, meaning that the designers and the shop share the financial uncertainty. This allows Berlinomat to take risks by showing more daring and experimental design. It's also good for the customers: you pay more than you would in a chain shop, but you know the item isn't a copy-of-a-copy, and that you're investing in a young and creative economy.

The Brandenburger Tor

HOTELS
MITTE

€ **The Club House Hostel** Kalkscheunenstraße 4–5, 28 09 79 79, www.clubhouse-berlin.de. A big common room and a 24-hour party atmosphere, a venue for performance, live music and parties. Singles €32, doubles €46, quads €20 and dorms €14. *U* to Oranienburger Tor **Map p. 8, 3B**

€€ **Honigmond** Invalidenstraße 122, 28 44 55 77, www.honigmond-berlin.de. Hotel in listed 1845 building, individually designed rooms with original wooden floorboards and antique furniture, and peaceful courtyard garden. Singles €89–109, doubles €109–159. *U* to Oranienburger Tor **Map p. 8, 3A**

Künstlerheim Luise Luisenstraße 19, 28 44 80, www.kuenstlerheim-luise.de. Built in 1825, each room has been designed by a different artist. Singles €82–95, doubles €79–139. **U** to Friedrichstraße **Map p. 8, 3B**

Hotel Taunus Monbijouplatz 1, 283 52 54, www.hotel-taunus.de. Direct on the Hackescher markt, this is as central as they come. Singles €88, doubles €99. Special offers during the summer. **S** to Hackescher Markt **Map p. 9, 1B**

€€€Artotel Wallstraße 70, 240 620, www.artotel.de. Paintings by Baselitz hang in this luxury hotel on the FischerInsel. It also has a good restaurant. Choose the colour of your room, ranging from €130–260. **U** to Märkisches Museum Friedrichshain **Map p. 9, 2C**

TIERGARTEN

€€€Grand Hyatt Marlene Dietrich Platz 2, 25 53 12 34, www.berlin. grand.hyatt.de. Five-star hotel on Potsdamerplatz, with spacious rooms, great views and a roof garden. Prices vary according to the time of year: a double costs €175 in summer and €250 in winter. Breakfast €22. **U** to Potsdamerplatz **Map p. 8, 2C**

Ritz Carlton Potsdamerplatz 3, 33 77 77, www.ritzcarlton.com. Empire-style foyer inside an Art Deco-esque shell, like a film set where the guests are extras walking around in jogging suits. Single rooms start at €250, doubles at €280 (€30 more during peak season), and go up from there. **Map p. 8, 2C**

CHARLOTTENBURG

€ **A&0 Hostel am Zoo** Joachimstalerstraße 1, 0800 222 5722, www.aohostels.com. Central west but far from the bar scene: singles €70, doubles €23, quad €18, dorm €15. Rates cheaper off season (summer). **U** to Zoologischergarten **Map p. 105, 2C**

€€ **Ku'damm 101 Hotel** Kurfürstendamm 101, 52 00 55 0, www.kudamm101.com. Modern and stylish with 170 rooms fitted out with state of the art communication technology, along with a 'wellness lounge'. Right on west Berlin's shopping mile. Singles €101, doubles €118, breakfast €13. **U** to Kurfürstendamm **Map p. 104, 3C**

Kurfürst Hotel-Pension Bleibtreustraße 34, 88 56 82 0, www.kurfuerst.de. Small and practical second storey hotel. Singles €72–77, doubles €92–97. **U** to Uhlandstraße **Map p. 105, 1C**

€€€Hotel Bleibtreu Bleibtreustraße 31, 88 47 40, www.bleibtreu.com. Luxury hotel with an adjoining restaurant and café. Singles from €142–€220 and doubles from €152–€232. *U* to Uhlandstraße **Map p. 105, 1C**

Hotel Brandenburger Hof Eislebenerstraße 14, 214 050, www.brandenburger-hof.de. Quality and elegantly designed hotel, with adjoining restaurant. Singles €170, doubles €210 and upwards. *U* to Augsburgerstraße, Kurfürstenstrasse **Map p. 105, 2C**

Kempinski Kurfürstendamm 27, 88 43 40. Kempinski, an institution on the Ku'damm. **Map p. 105, 1C**

Q! Berlin Knesebeckstraße 67, 810 006 0, www.loock-hotels.com. New hotel with futuristic design that is still warm and welcoming. Singles from €140, doubles €150, with reductions offers according to the time of year. Breakfast €18. **Map p. 105, 1C**

Savoy Fasanenstraße 9–10, 31 10 30, www.hotel-savoy.com. Thomas Mann's favourite Berlin hotel. To this day it sets standards in comfort and elegance. Singles €142–222, doubles €152–232, suite €202–292. Breakfast €15. *U* to Uhlandstraße **Map p. 105, 1C**

KREUZBERG

€€ East-Side Hotel Mühlenstraße 6, 29 38 33, www.eastside cityhotel.de. Dockside location with views of the wall. Young and informal hotel with small rooms. Singles €60–80, doubles €70–80. *U* to Warschauerstrasse **Map p. 133, 3A**

art glossary

Baselitz, Georg (1938–) Moved to West Berlin in 1956 after being thrown out of art school in East Berlin for 'social political immaturity'. In 1961 exhibited and wrote the *Pandemoniac Manifesto* with painter Eugen Schönbeck; in 1963 his paintings were confiscated from an exhibition at a Berlin gallery because of 'obscenity'. Baselitz was influenced by the writings of Kandinsky and Malevitch, as well as the philosophy of Artaud and Nietzsche. He was the leading exponent of 'new figuration', a reaction against the dominance of painterly abstraction during the 1950s. In the early 1970s he began hanging his paintings upside down in an attempt to break the constraints of the pictorial frame. His paintings can be seen in the Neue Nationalgalerie (see p. 82) and the Berlinische Galerie (see p. 134).

Beckmann, Max (1884–1950) Joined the **Berliner Secession** in 1904—like other members, was much influenced by Impressionism. Served as a medic during WWI but was discharged after one year after suffering a breakdown. Post-war he began combining mythical and allegorical subjects with social criticism and became allied to '*Neue Sachlichkeit*'. National Socialism was hostile to Beckmann and included him in the '*Entartete Kunst*' exhibition of 1937. He moved to Amsterdam, where he remained throughout the war. In 1947 he emigrated to the US. Beckmann's work can be seen in the Alte Nationalgalerie (see p. 28), the Neue Nationalgalerie (see p. 82) and the Berlinische Galerie (see p. 143).

Berliner Secession During the 1890s, groups formed in Vienna, Munich and Berlin that, in response to French Impressionism, began to break away from academic traditions. The Berlin Secession was founded by **Max Liebermann**, and included **Lovis Corinth**, Max Slevogt and **Heinrich Zille**. In 1910 the '*Neue Secession*' was founded by Max Pechstein for Expressionist artists who themselves had been rejected by the Secession. Works can be seen in the Alte Nationalgalerie (see p. 28), and the Neue Secession in the Berlinische Galerie (see p. 134).

Beuys, Joseph (1921–1986) While serving as a fighter pilot during WWII, Beuys was shot down over the Crimea. He was rescued by peasants who wrapped him in felt and dressed his wounds with tallow; these materials became major elements of his work, which was based around the principles of 'social plasticity'. His work is in the collection at the Hamburger Bahnhof (see p. 89).

Biedermeier (1815–50) A style typified by domesticity, urbanity and the love of order, a rejection of the sentimentality of Romanticism. In interior design, Biedermeier combined elements of the French Empire style with English utilitarianism, and can be seen in the Knoblauchhaus (see p. 41). In painting, the Biedermeier spirit is represented by Karl Spitzweg and Georg Waldmüller, whose work can be seen in the Alte Nationalgalerie (see p. 34).

Blechen, Carl (1798–1840) Romantic landscape artist and 'master of light'; Blechen admired Turner and Friedrich and was an influence on Berlin naturalists, including Adolf Menzel, although Blechen himself only gained full recognition posthumously. Works by Blechen can be seen in the Alte Nationalgalerie (see p. 33) and New Pavilion of the Schloss Charlottenburg (see p. 106).

Böcklin, Arnold (1827–1910) A Neo-Romantic Swiss painter most famous for the *Island of Death*, Böcklin was an influence on Symbolist and Surrealist painters. He populated his naturalistic landscapes with mythological creatures and infused them with his obsession with death. His images were some of the most popular of the fin de siècle period. Works by Böcklin can be seen in the Alte Nationalgalerie (see p. 35).

Corinth, Lovis (1858–1925) Painter of many styles and a conduit for international ideas into Germany. A 'Neo-idealist', painting scenes from literature and history in a realistic style, Corinth came to Berlin from Prussia in 1900 and joined the **Berliner Secession**. He is remarkable for his technique of 'drawing with paint', which became ever more agitated after his stroke in 1911. Too naturalistic for the modernists, Corinth was blacklisted by museums. Works by Corinth can be seen in the Alte Nationalgalerie (see p. 38).

Cranach, Lucas (Cranach the Elder) (1472–1553) Renaissance painter and humanist famous for his sensual nudes. Court painter to the Electors of Saxony in Wittenberg and friend of Martin Luther, he was also a propagandist for Protestantism. Works by Cranach can be seen in the Gemäldegalerie (see p. 73).

Dix, Otto (1891–1969) A survivor of the Somme, Dix became a vehement social critic during the 1920s and 1930s. His realistic style, aimed at the general viewer, caricatured the cripples, prostitutes and profiteers of the Weimar Republic. Later Dix turned to a more restrained style in the face of the increasingly reactionary National Socialist government. Works by Dix can be seen in the Neue Nationalgalerie (see p. 86) and the Berlinische Galerie (see p. 134).

Dürer, Albrecht (1471–1528) Prolific painter and engraver whose career bridged the late Gothic and the Renaissance periods. Though based in Nuremberg, Dürer's travels brought him into contact with the leading Italian painters, above all Bellini. Works by Dürer can be seen in the Gemäldegalerie (see p. 70).

Entartete Kunst (Degenerate Art) This was the title given to an exhibition in Munich in 1937 of 650 of 16,000 works of modern art confiscated by the National Socialists. The exhibition toured the country until 1941 and altogether around three million visitors saw it. 'Degenerate Art' included Impressionism, Expressionism, Surrealism, Dada and *Neue Sachlichkeit*. In the exhibition the works were displayed alongside drawings by and photos of the mentally and physically handicapped. There were concurrent dismissals in museums and academies, as well as bans on individual artists; the term was applied also to film, theatre, architecture and music. Works by the some of the artists included can be seen in the Alte Nationalgalerie (see p. 24), the Neue Nationalgalerie (see p. 82) and the Berlinische Galerie (see p. 134).

Friedrich, Caspar David (1774–1840) Romantic painter responsible for making landscape a subject, not a backdrop. Friedrich's famous advice to artists was to 'close your bodily eye, so you may see your picture first with your spiritual eye'. The exaggerated scenery with the trademark *Rückenfigur* (figures with their backs turned) were intended to stimulate the experience of communion with God, who Friedrich believed revealed himself through nature. Paintings by Friedrich can be seen in the New Pavilion of the Schloss Charlottenburg (see p. 112) and the Alte Nationalgalerie (see pp. 33–34).

Grosz, George (1893–1959) Berlin Dadaist known at the time as the 'Propagandada' for his illustrations in John Heartfield's Dada magazine. Discharged from the army during WWI on mental health grounds, Grosz developed a style which subverted Analytic Cubism into fragmentation and chaos. His 'critical realism' earned him several court appearances for public insult. Grosz moved to the US in 1932, where he lost his critical edge, or as he put it: 'repressed everything in me that seemed too Grosz-like'. Works by Grosz can be seen in the Neue Nationalgalerie (see p. 86) and the Berlinische Galerie (see p. 138).

Gründerzeit A period of rapid economic and industrial growth built on French reparation following France's loss to Germany in 1871. This was also the time of the formation of the German Reich, achieved through the 'blood and iron' rule of Chancellor Otto von Bismarck. In design the Gründerzeit favoured historicism; Neo-Renaissance was dominant until **Jugendstil** in 1900. You can see the remnants in Kreuzberg and Charlottenburg.

Jugendstil German Art Nouveau, or Jugendstil, sought to replace historicism with a modern style at the turn of the 20th C. Its effect was particularly revolutionary in Germany, where design and architecture was dominated by the monumentality of the imperial aesthetic. Developing in the applied arts, Jugendstil was at first characterised by curved and abstract forms taken from the plant world. Later it became more geometric, and by around 1910 had become Art Deco.

Junge Wilde In the early 1980s, group of young West Berlin artists launched the 'Critical Realist' movement. The paintings of the Junge Wilde were bright and loosely painted and took their subject matter from the pubs and clubs of Kreuzberg, a district where studios were cheap and the counter-culture flourished.

Artists associated with the movement include Rainer Fetting and Helmut Middendorf, whose work can be seen at the Berlinische Galerie (see p. 134).

Kiefer, Anselm (1945–) Painter and sculptor renowned for tackling issues of modern German history. He developed a style that can be called 'Neo-Expressionist', using unconventional materials such as lead, straw, earth and blood. Works by Kiefer can be seen in the Hamburger Bahnhof (see p. 91).

Knobelsdorff, Georg Wenzeslaus von (1683–1757) Architect to Friedrich II, famous for the Sanssouci Palace and the new wing of the Schloss Charlottenburg (see p. 106), both of which are masterpieces of European Rococo. Other buildings include the Neue Synagoge on Oranienburgerstraße (see p. 40).

Kollwitz, Käthe (1867–1945) Berlin graphic artist whose social-political subject matter was influenced by the death of her son in WWI. Though aligned with the Dadaists politically, her compassionate realism set her apart from the group artistically. She was a professor at the Academy of Art in Berlin but was dismissed by the National Socialists. Kollwitz' husband was murdered by the National Socialists for his political convictions and she died near Dresden shortly before the end of the war. Works by Kollwitz can be seen in the Käthe Kollwitz Museum in Charlottenburg (see p. 120).

Langhans, Carl Gotthard (1732–1808) Court architect to Friedrich Wilhelm II, famous for the Belvedere at Schloss Charlottenburg and the Brandenburger Tor (see pp. 112 and 97). The leading architect of his time, his building career mirrors the transition from late Baroque to early Classicism.

Liebermann, Max (1847–1935) Painter and graphic artist who favoured social themes, known as the 'German Impressionist'. As founder of the **Berliner Secession**, Liebermann was responsible for bringing German art away from genre painting, though he came to be regarded as old-fashioned by the Expressionists. Works by Liebermann can be seen in the Alte Nationalgalerie (see p. 28).

Menzel, Adolph (1815–1905) Self-taught painter who learned his trade in the lithographic workshop of his father. He became the darling of the Prussian court, painting scenes from the life of Friedrich the Great. During a spell in France he discovered the Impressionists. On his return to Berlin he applied the same realism to pictures of industrial growth. Works by Menzel can be seen at Schloss Charlottenburg (see p. 106) and the Alte Nationalgalerie (see p. 38).

Neue Sachlichkeit New Objectivity is a term used to describe an exhibition of contemporary German art held in 1925. It was characterised by left-wing politics and an interest in depicting everyday life. The style's exponents include **Otto Dix**, **George Grosz** and Christian Schad. *Neue Sachlichkeit* came to end with the cultural pessimism brought on by the world economic crisis and the rise of National Socialism.

Pesne, Antoine (1683–1757) French-born court portrait painter to Friedrich I, Friedrich Wilhelm I and Friedrich II. His work shows the transition from the late Baroque to the Rococo, and is celebrated for its delicate flesh tones. Paintings by Pesne can be seen at Schloss Charlottenburg (see p. 106) and the Gemäldegalerie (see p. 70).

Stiftung Preußicher Kulturbesistz (SPK) SPK, or the Prussian cultural heritage foundation, oversees sixteen museums. It was established in 1957 and grew to include institutions from the former GDR after reunification.

Rococo Style that emerged in France around 1700 and spread throughout Europe, characterised by fragile, supple and organic forms in pastel pinks, blues and greens. The style was taken up eagerly by Friedrich the Great: Knobelsdorff's design for the Golden Gallery at Schloss Charlottenburg (see p. 111) is a highlight. Rococo painters collected by Friedrich include Watteau in Schloss Charlottenburg and Claude Lorraine in the Gemäldegalerie (see p. 70).

Romanticism Also known as the *Goethezeit*; it began in Germany around 1800 and ended half a century later. Represented in painting by **Caspar David Friedrich**, **Karl Friedrich Schinkel** and

Philipp Otto Runge. In its philosophical expression Romanticism prioritised the spiritual over the material; in arts and architecture it revived the Gothic style. Politically, German Romanticism was associated with national unity and strength after the defeat of the French during the Napoleonic wars.

Schadow, Johann Gottfried (1764–1850) Court sculptor under Friedrich Wilhelm III, director of the Berlin Academy of Art and contemporary of Schinkel. He was influenced by Italian Classicism (Schadow produced a sculpture of the queen wrapped only in a thin drape, which the king forbade to be shown in public). Schadow made the Quadriga atop the Brandenburger Tor; his work can also be seen in the Friedrichswerdesche Kirche (see p. 42) and in the Alte Nationalgalerie (see p. 33).

Scharoun, Hans (1893–1972) Modernist architect, famous for the Philarmonie at Potsdamer Platz (1956–63). Also the architect of the Staatsbibliothek on Potsdamer Platz (see p. 96), which appears in Wim Wenders' film *Wings of Desire*.

Schinkel, Karl Friedrich (1781–1841) Court architect under Friedrich Wilhelm III. His buildings include the Altes Museum (see p. 23) and the Friedrichswerdesche Kirche (see p. 42). The Classicist Schinkel was not only prolific but also incredibly versatile; he built houses, stately homes, museums and churches, and was a painter, interior designer and set designer. His furniture can be seen at Schloss Charlottenburg (see p. 106) and his paintings in the Alte Nationalgalerie (see p. 28).

Zille, Heinrich (1858–1929) From a working class family, Berliner Zille studied lithography in evening classes. In 1901 his work was shown in an exhibition on the Berliner Secession. His subject matter was the proletariat, whom he portrayed lovingly and critically, bringing out tenderness and lewdness in equal measure. Immensely popular with the general public, he was also appointed professor of the Prussian Academy of Art. Zille's photography, which shows a high degree of modernity, was discovered only after his death, and can be seen at the Berlinische Galerie (see p. 134). His prints and drawings can be seen at the Zille Museum in the Nikolai Viertel in Mitte (see p. 41).

index

art/shop/eat Berlin
First edition 2005
Published by Blue Guides Limited, a Somerset Books company
The Studio, 51 Causton St., London SWIP 4AT

ISBN 0-905131-05-4

Published in the United States of America by
WW Norton & Company, Inc
500 Fifth Avenue, New York, NY 10110, USA

ISBN 0-393-32785-X

Series devised by Gemma Davies   Editor: Maya Mirsky
Layout and production: Anikó Kuzmich   Copy editing: Mark Griffith
Photo editor: Hadley Kincade

Floorplans by Imre Bába, ©Blue Guides Limited
Maps by Dimap Bt., ©Blue Guides Limited

Printed and bound in China by SunFung Offset Binding Co.,Ltd.

Front cover: *Akt im Atelier (Norilein)/Sitzender Akt mit Erhobenen Armen* by Ernst
Ludwig Kirchner, ©Dr. Wolfgang and Ingeborg Henze-Ketterer, Wichtrach/Bern. In
the Staatliche Museen zu Berlin - Preußischer Kulturbesitz, Neue Nationalgalerie,
Photo by Jörg P. Anders. Back cover: Reichstag dome, photo by Hadley Kincade

For permission to reproduce pictures throughout the book, grateful thanks are due to
the following: Staatliche Museen zu Berlin - Preußischer Kulturbesitz,
Vorderasiatisches Museum, photo by Reinhard Saczewski (p. 22); Staatliche Museen
zu Berlin - Preußischer Kulturbesitz, Alte Nationalgalerie, photo by Andres Kilger (p.
34); Staatliche Museen zu Berlin - Preußischer Kulturbesitz, Gemäldegalerie, photo
by Jörg P. Anders (p. 73); ©Dr. Wolfgang and Ingeborg Henze-Ketterer,
Wichtrach/Bern. In the Staatliche Museen zu Berlin - Preußischer Kulturbesitz,
Neue Nationalgalerie, Photo by Jörg P. Anders (p. 84); ©DACS 2004, courtesy of the
Brücke Museum (p. 123); ©DACS 2004, courtesy of the Berlinische Galerie,
Landesmuseum für Moderne Kunst, Fotografie und Architektur (p. 137); ©DACS
2004, courtesy of the Galerie Vostell (p. 168)

Photographs by Sebastian Hanel (pp. 43, 95, 173) and Hadley Kincade (pp. 10, 40, 45,
46,56, 61, 65, 66, 83, 98, 99, 107, 121, 140, 147, 160, 166, 179, 185, 190, 194)